DO
EXPLORERS
WEAR
SOCKS?

DO EXPLORERS WEAR SOCKS?

Carolyn Ellis

With Illustrations by Susanna Theron

THE CAMEL Doc!

© Carolyn Ellis, 2022

Published by Carolyn Ellis

All rights reserved. No part of this book may be reproduced, adapted, stored in a retrieval system or transmitted by any means, electronic, mechanical, photocopying, or otherwise without the prior written permission of the author.

The rights of Carolyn Ellis to be identified as the author of this work have been asserted in accordance with the Copyright, Designs and Patents Act 1988.

A CIP catalogue record for this book is available from the British Library.

ISBN 978-1-7390823-0-7

Book layout by Clare Brayshaw

Prepared and printed by:

York Publishing Services Ltd
64 Hallfield Road
Layerthorpe
York YO31 7ZQ

Tel: 01904 431213

Website: www.yps-publishing.co.uk

Special Message Just For You

Dear Reader,
Are you sure you meant to pick this book?
WARNING... it's only for brave people.
IF that's you, keep reading.
You are going on a REAL desert adventure!
This epic journey sets off to make the world's first ever crossing of a desert in China.
It involves humans from three very different cultures, thirty awesome camels and, as you would expect, a lot of SAND!
In the desert it gets extremely hot and freezing cold... and, of course, we run out of water.

It's a TRUE story: a real-life adventure.

Things are going to get very tough.
You might become thirsty, so fill up your water bottle before you start reading. When we get sandstorms, you are going to need goggles (sunglasses will do), and a scarf to wrap around

your face. At all times you will need a compass so you know where you are and can find your friends. A torch is a good idea. Ideally, one that goes on your head so your hands are free for doing all sorts of things from loading camels to writing in your diaries.

YOU are coming with me. I am the team medic, my nickname is the 'Camel Doc' and I really want to share my story with you.

We start off with a dramatic and rather horrid story involving maggots... be brave... keep reading. Things do improve!

*Then I need to tell you a few facts just so you know where we are, how we got there and what we were trying to do. When a word is written in **BOLD** writing, it means you can flick to the back of the book and learn more. Where you see this: 📷 you can go online to the see the original photo taken on the expedition.*

When things go wrong (and they do) you may ask yourself, 'Why don't they just use their mobiles to ring for help?' Things were different when this expedition took place. Can you believe we didn't have mobile phones? The type we all have today didn't exist! Possibly that's a scary thought for you; in fact, it's a scary thought for me now!

Remember this is a TRUE STORY and YOU are now part of it.

I really hope you enjoy it and that it will inspire you to follow your dreams.
A journey of a thousand miles quite literally starts with one step, so we'd better get started. Good luck and, most importantly, have fun!
Lots of love,

'The CAMEL DOC' XX

For further info, lots of real photos and games visit www.thecameldoc.com

CHAPTER 1

Maggots Hitch a Ride

A straw-coloured liquid ran down the hind leg of one of the camels and dripped onto the desert floor.

Three weeks into the expedition, things started to go wrong. It was bitterly cold, the sun was blocked out by dust and, worst of all, something was wrong with the camels.

We had been walking for eight hours every day. Charles limped – an old knee injury playing up, but he didn't want to talk about it, choosing to 'soldier on' using a gnarly old branch as a walking stick.

The camels worried me more.

Rupert discovered an ominous discharge coming from under one of the saddles. He told Charles what he had found.

That night as we staggered into camp with yet another storm brewing, Charles shouted through the noise of whirling sand.

'Remove all saddles. We need to find out what is going on with the camels. Our lives depend on them!'

Everyone started to unload the camels and for the first time in weeks removed the saddles. Rupert and I carefully inspected every camel. It was not good news.

There were huge wounds caused by poor loading and inadequate padding under the saddle. Deep cuts had formed where ropes sliced into their flesh.

Camels are strong, stoic animals; complaining is not in their nature.

How had we let this happen?

WARNING: If you are a bit squeamish you might want to skip through the next bit.

The deep lacerations on our poor camels' humps were infested and crawling with wriggly, white, fat MAGGOTS!

I had a bad feeling. I knew who was going to have to deal with this.

Charles peered at the wounds, went a bit green and said, 'The person closest to a vet will have to sort out this mess.'

Now who could that be?

Yep, you've guessed it – the team medic... ME.

Looking around at all the men making faces, pretending to be sick and making comments like, 'Oh, yeeeeuk, that's revolting' it was pretty obvious I was going to have to do it!

I had been a nurse in the army and faced all sorts of challenges, although I do admit, I had never removed maggots from hairy camels before!

I found the camel sack marked with a red cross and pulled out my medical kit.

What on earth do you need to operate on a camel? I delved into the medical box, not really sure what I was looking for.

Eventually I produced some dark liquid for cleaning wounds, a sharp scalpel (a surgeon's knife) and some long tweezers. I smiled, waved them in the air and tried to look confident.

The camel-handlers and Rupert rounded up the injured animals and, after quite a bit of bellowing, and I don't mean from Rupert, the camels were persuaded to sit down. Understandably frightened, wild-eyed and frothing at the mouth, the first camel reluctantly let me inspect his wounds. I took a deep breath and looked around at the gathered crowd. The men and the camels were watching my every move.

This was a TEST.

Was the one woman on the trip really capable of sorting out this rather revolting mess?

There was no time to be squeamish. Come on, you can do this. Show them all what you're made of. After all, wounds are wounds... aren't they?

Before starting to probe into the holes, I negotiated with Charles. 'I must be allowed water to wash my hands after treating the camels!' (A reasonable request don't you think?) Except you need to remember that on desert expeditions you only have water for drinking!

No water should be used for washing or even brushing your teeth!!

The smell of infection and rotting flesh was revolting.

You might have smelt something similar on a hot summer's day when you walk past bins that haven't been emptied for two weeks! Although I don't expect you stop and look inside, unfortunately for me, that was just what I had to do...

I rolled up my sleeves... 'Here goes.'

It was an odd and unusual feeling, putting my hand inside a camel's warm, wobbly, hairy hump! Gently, I explored the wound, located the infected areas, made small incisions to release pus, cut away dead tissue and removed the horrid maggots. Interestingly, maggots will usually only eat rotting dead flesh and actually do try to clean wounds. But I still didn't like them. It must have been an unpleasant feeling for the camels, so I took the decision to get rid of the maggots. 'Sorry, maggots, but you are not welcome here.' I scattered them on the desert floor. They wriggled off. If I am honest, I didn't care what happened to them. I was, however, worried about our camels, especially now that it was my job to look after them. From that day onwards, every evening before my open-air people clinic, I first conducted a much more important camel clinic!

When grownups are ill and they go to the doctor's, they sometimes get a sick note, which means they are excused working for a few days while they get better. Our camels needed sick notes. I told Charles that the camels with deep wounds must not carry loads. Good news for the poorly camels but not so good for the fit ones which now had to carry even more! Charles, standing some distance away (he didn't like maggots or the smell) shouted to me, 'I've got a great nickname for you, Carolyn... from now on, you will be known as the 'CAMEL DOC.'

So now you know how I got my nickname. But to find out what I was doing in a vast desert on the other side of the world and the one female on an expedition, we will need to go back to the unlikely beginning... a bowl of porridge in Scotland.

CHAPTER 2

How It All Began

I was in Scotland eating a lovely steaming bowl of healthy porridge for my breakfast when 'JBS' (Colonel **John Blashford-Snell)** announced that he needed to be back in London... tonight! I had been driving him around Great Britain, together we were speaking at schools. Our talk was called 'Life of Adventure', and we were encouraging young people like you to think about all the adventures they could have in the world.

By the time we arrived in central London it was late afternoon. I parked the car outside a smart hotel.

JBS got out, leaned back in and said, 'You must come tonight and meet Ran.'

('Ran to his friends, Sir **Ranulph Fiennes** to you and me.') 'You never know, it might open some new doors for you.' Little did I know that many years later it would open a particularly large and heavy door!

Friday night in London and a talk by an explorer or party with friends?... ummmm, that's a tough one.

What would you choose?

A big part of me wanted to see my pals, but then a little voice somewhere inside my head said, 'Go to the talk. It might change your life.' A bit dramatic, I agree, but that was pretty much what happened.

It didn't look very promising as I walked into the room where people were having drinks before the lecture. I was the youngest by a long way and one of very few women.

The men were quite elderly, serious, and dressed in dark suits – really quite dull, and none of them looked anything like Indiana Jones, or **Bear Grylls**!! I knew it!

Should have gone partying with my friends.

Although meeting Sir Ranulph was a great privilege. He really is one of the greatest polar explorers of all time.

You might be interested to know that he was nervous about giving his talk, making him, I think, reassuringly normal. I get nervous before I give a talk.

I expect you get a bit scared too if you have to read or talk in front of your classmates. Next time, just remember that even GREAT EXPLORERS get frightened sometimes.

Arriving late and slightly flustered was a man more my age, still in a boring suit, with wild blond hair and a smiley face. By chance we ended up sitting next to each other and so began a friendship that would change my life.

With a magician's flourish, he produced a silk handkerchief from the pocket of his boring suit. Strangely, it had a map of the **Taklamakan Desert** on it.

I wasn't sure what to make of this guy. I mean, who has a hanky with a map of a desert on it?

A bit strange.

Before I knew it, he was excitedly telling me about his idea: an expedition to make the world's first ever west/east crossing of a desert in China. A thousand miles of sand dunes and extreme weather – very, very hot and freezing cold. He would lead a team of British and Chinese explorers and a lot of CAMELS!

Oh, and did I tell you it's known by the local people as the DESERT OF DEATH and the DESERT OF NO RETURN?

How could anyone in their right mind think that trying to cross that desert was a good idea?

The guy with the wild blond hair was called Charles – he was a soldier in the British Army who loved adventure and doing exciting things that no one had done before.

I had been a captain in the **Queen Alexandra's Royal Army Nursing Corps** and provided medical support on expeditions all over the world. Charles needed an experienced team medic. He also knew that a woman on the trip would be an advantage.

1. More interest from TV, media etc. (women doing these things was unusual back then).

2. More sponsorship.

Companies that might offer support either in the form of money or equipment wanted to see equal opportunities. For example, one of our sponsors, a famous British biscuit manufacturer, didn't want to see only boys eating their biscuits. We all love biscuits... even camels love to nibble them. I will tell you more about that later.

The world of expeditions and adventures in 1992 was still dominated by men. Why shouldn't women get a chance to do challenging and dangerous things?

Strangely, and I have no idea why, I wanted to!

I remember being at home in Devon enjoying a delicious Sunday roast with my mother and brothers.

During the meal, I casually announced, 'Oh, have I told you? I am off to China next year to cross the Desert of Death, also known as the Desert of No Return.'

No one seemed that surprised. I think my mother said something like, 'That's interesting, dear.' My brothers probably heard, 'Desert of NO RETURN' and thought, 'Good, she will be gone for a while!'

From a smart London office loaned by an oil company Charles talked to lots of people that wanted to go on his trip. He needed to find the very best. **Turn to page 311 for pictures of the team.**

Let me introduce a few of the successful candidates.

Barney, one of Charles' best friends, was a soldier in the army. He was in charge of the support team. If things went wrong, it was Barney's job to try to save us.

Richard had worked in the **foreign office** and spoke **Mandarin** fluently. He was really good at helping people from different countries learn to get on together. He tried to stop people disagreeing by helping them listen and understand each other.

Rupert had been a soldier in the Parachute Regiment.

He was a skilled radio operator and navigator.

When I say radio operator, I don't mean he turned the radio on and we listened to Radio 1…

He used a device which allowed us to communicate with our friends in the support team.

Mark had also been in the army and attended university in Beijing. He joined the team as radio operator, navigator and translator. Later in the expedition we found out that he was also a brilliant story teller.

More team members will be introduced as we go along.

In Western China, in the office of the Xinjiang travel company, Mr Gou, a senior official, held his head in his hands and wondered how on earth he would find thirty camels capable of walking a thousand miles.

In oasis towns on the Southern **Silk Road, Uyghur** (pronounced WE GAR), families living on the edge of the desert heard the news that a team led by a British explorer wanted to attempt the world's first crossing of their desert.

I think I need to give you some information about the Taklamakan desert. That's 'desert' and not 'dessert', the tasty thing you eat! A young friend of mine read this book and thought it said 'dessert of no return.'

She thought her dessert would be taken away and not brought back... that would not be good.

So, are we all clear it's 'deSert' (the sandy thing) and not 'deSSert', the tasty chocolatey ice creamy delicious thing?

Some important information:

The Taklamakan Desert is a vast sandy desert in Northwest China in the Xinjiang province.

To give you some idea of size, the whole area is bigger than the United Kingdom. Go to the website for a map of where the desert is. Taklamakan means 'Desert of DEATH. You go in but you never come out.' Obviously, we hoped that was not true. The fact you are reading this story means at least one of us made it out, but what happened along the way? There were many stories and legends of the people who had lived there and tales of explorers from hundreds of years ago, but there was no record of the desert ever being crossed from West to East. In 1895, the Swedish explorer, **Sven Hedin**, ventured into the desert and found treasures from a forgotten Buddhist civilisation. His expedition ran out of water and two of the Uyghur camel-handlers and seven of the eight camels died of thirst. Sven Hedin saved the life of one of his camel-handlers by carrying water to him. He had nothing to transport the water in so filled up his waterproof boots! You would have to be pretty thirsty to drink from Sven's old boots. He had worn them for many years on expeditions all over the world. Kasim, the camel-handler, was brave and very, very thirsty; he drank the water from the boots and lived to tell the tale! We DO NOT want to repeat that experience drinking from someone's old boot! NO, THANK YOU!

CHAPTER 3

Support From The Queen's Husband

You can't just go to a country like China and say, 'Hey, we've come to walk across your desert, and could you give us some camels to carry our bags?'

No, that would not work.

Charles spent several years of careful planning and attended lots of meetings with the British and Chinese governments, seeking special permission to be allowed to attempt the crossing. He built a strong friendship with the wonderful Mr Guo, who ran an adventure travel company in China. Mr Guo was the leader of the Chinese team. He also helped find thirty **BACTRIAN CAMELS**.

Expeditions are like long, exciting but dangerous holidays. They cost thousands of pounds. The year before we left, all team members were involved in trying to raise money and find supplies. It was not easy.

Why would any company or sponsor want to be associated with an expedition that was quite likely to end in disaster?

The headline news could easily be:

'BRITISH EXPLORERS DIE OF THIRST IN INFAMOUS DESERT.'

Somehow, we needed to convince people that we had a good chance of making it out alive.

Unfortunately, the name of the desert was not helping.

*DESERT OF DEATH,
DESERT OF NO RETURN.*

I think you would agree it didn't sound very promising!

We wrote letters (no emails back then) to everyone from oil to water companies, biscuit makers, clothes manufacturers, food suppliers (especially CHOCOLATE makers), communication companies, (TV, radio etc.) and wealthy eccentric individuals.

We knocked on doors and tried to get meetings with people. It was tough; not many people shared our vision or enthusiasm.

Understandably, some bosses of big companies looked at us as if we were completely bonkers and, if I am honest, I could see their point. 'Desert of DEATH,' why would you want to go there?

We desperately needed some important people to support us.

The Queen's husband, Prince Phillip, and a retired Prime Minister, came to our rescue as they strangely believed in us!

People and companies then thought, 'OK, so the Queen's husband thinks they can make it, we will support them.'

Some gave money, others provided much-needed equipment, some supplied food and, best of all, some gave us lots of bars of CHOCOLATE! Ok so it might melt but let's worry about that later.

I am not going to list all the amazing companies and people that helped us, but as we go across the desert you will see and hear about many of them.

You might even eat some of them… that's the food: not the sponsors!

Interest in our expedition grew, and I was interviewed by national newspapers and photographed running over Dartmoor with my dogs.

There was a lot of work to be done. We researched previous explorers' unsuccessful trips and looked at maps and satellite images taken by **NASA.** We studied weather patterns, gathered equipment, food and, most importantly, got ourselves extremely fit.

My training included running over the moors every day with my lurchers, Pip and Tess. I tried desperately to keep up. If dogs could laugh, they would have howled with laughter at my efforts.

I carried a heavy rucksack and wore the boots I intended to use in the desert. Farmers in tractors and friends driving over the moors tooted their horns as they spotted me. I hopped and jumped over bracken and heather, usually in swirling mist and pouring rain. Not the best preparation for a dry, HOT desert. To help acclimatise myself for the heat, I exercised in a gym wearing lots of jumpers and a hat. People must have thought 'she's bonkers,' as I sweated buckets but refused to take off any layers!

My local TV company, West Country television, filmed and interviewed me. A recurrent question was, 'Do you think you will die?' NO!

I may be a bit odd, but not even I would go on a trip if I really thought yep, you are going to DIE!

One of the scariest things I did before the expedition was go on a live chat show for BBC Radio 4.

Let me try to explain what it was like.

The black London taxi dropped me outside Broadcasting House which is the headquarters of the BBC. Feeling incredibly nervous, I gazed up at the imposing grey building and felt about the size of an ant. I thought of those famous explorers being nervous before they gave lectures. I was not a famous explorer. I wanted to run away!

Pull yourself together!

Be BRAVE, you can do this.

NO running away!

I slowly climbed the steps and reported to reception.

A lady smiled and said, 'Follow me.'

Suddenly, she was off. Almost running, I tried to keep up. We whizzed along dark, narrow corridors, down stairs and down again. Golly, we are a long way underground! Every now and then my guide pointed to various doors with lights outside that glowed red into the darkness 'ON AIR.'

She put a finger to her lips. I needed to be quiet. I wondered about the famous people inside. Perhaps Radio 1 DJs?

NO stopping. My guide sped on.

I was oblivious to the fact that within minutes I too would be live 'ON AIR.'

We arrived at our destination. A room with coffee and lots of yummy doughnuts. (It's funny what you remember.) I was introduced to other guests and briefly to the show's host. There was no time for me to be starstruck. **LIBBY PURVES** pointed to a chair. I sat down, smiled nervously, and thought, 'I will open my mouth to speak and nothing will come out!'

I watched in silence, feeling the colour drain from my face as we were counted down – 3, 2, 1. The studio crew pointed to a light that suddenly beamed RED. 'ON AIR.' We were live. Anything said now would be heard by thousands of listeners at home and in their cars. Eleven million people listen to Radio 4 each week. I hoped they were not all listening today. The other guests were very interesting a famous actor, a musician and a chef, the interviewer Libby knew all about each of us, and asked questions to keep us talking. Of course, the famous actor was good at talking, and kindly pretended to be interested in my stories asking me nice questions.

I was beginning to enjoy myself and managed to forget about the thousands of people listening.

My voice did work. According to my mother, I sounded good (but then she would say that!). Libby closed the show by saying, 'Carolyn, I hope you will come back to tell us stories about the desert, the men and the CAMELS!' Everyone apart from me laughed!

I was quickly learning that when you mention CAMELS, people go, 'Oooh! Horrid creatures that kick and SPIT and have foul smelling breath!' (Nice!) I hoped this was not entirely true!

I said, 'I would love to come back and tell you all how we got on crossing the desert, and that perhaps not all camels are bad.'

Everyone laughed again and wished me GOOD LUCK!

I had the distinct feeling they didn't think we were going to make it!

CHAPTER 4

How Many Pairs Of Socks?

What do you pack for your summer holiday?

It's quite difficult, isn't it, trying to decide what to take and what to leave behind.

Imagine packing for a three-month trip to a country you have never been to before where the temperature goes from ridiculously hot to arctic freezing!

How many pairs of socks? And underwear?

DO EXPLORERS WEAR SOCKS and underwear?

All will be revealed (not literally) later in the story.

On my expeditions, I always packed one special small parcel at the bottom of my rucksack, only to be opened in the event of disaster (meaning things aren't going well, we might not make it, and I need something to cheer me up!) I will tell you what was in it later, but have a think about what you might pack in your emergency bag.

If I was opening this parcel, one of two things had happened:

1. The expedition was over. (Hooray! We've made it!)

2. Things had gone terribly wrong!

The more expeditions I did, the fewer things I packed, especially as far as medical kit was concerned. I had learnt what was likely to go wrong, and realistically, what I would be able to do about it.

Rather worryingly, many people, including some of the world's top explorers, believed our journey would end in disaster. You know how you feel when someone says you won't be able to do something? It makes you even more determined. You think to yourself, 'YOU don't know me or what I am capable of.'

Time to show those doubters.

Arriving at Heathrow Airport, we were shocked to be surrounded by lots of photographers (paparazzi) waving cameras with very long lenses at us, like the ones you see at football matches, and film crews with fluffy microphones on sticks.

They jostled and pushed each other to interview and photograph us. It was all very odd and we hadn't expected it.

I was wearing my Aussie Outback bush hat, not because I thought I must look like an explorer, but because it would be crushed in my rucksack! However, it did rather add to the image of the eccentric British explorers.

We waved goodbye to our families and the camera crews and boarded the plane, first to

Hong Kong (HK). We sat together and looked relatively normal until the daily newspapers were handed around. Guess who was on the back page running across the moors with her dogs? 📷

Fellow passengers read about our trip, turned round in their seats, and looked and pointed at us. The cabin crew surprised us with glasses of champagne as the pilot made a special announcement over the tannoy and wished us all good luck.

Everyone on the plane cheered and clapped.

It was really happening!
We were on our way!

CHAPTER 5

Spicy Noodles For Breakfast

'Who needs the Desert of Death? I am going to die in a plane crash!'

I gripped the arm of the seat and stared out at the bright lights of HONG KONG (HK). Something wasn't right because we appeared to be flying down a street between skyscrapers!

ARE WE CRASHING?

THEN I remembered a friend's warning. She had told me to expect to fly very close to buildings.

She was not wrong.

I was looking straight into people's flats!

No joke, there were people showering and eating their breakfast. Was that **Granny Ola** or porridge they were tucking into?

We touched down safely on a short runway. The pilot warned us about a plane with its wheels off the tarmac and half in the sea! Luckily, all the passengers were ok; the plane just ran out of runway! For those of you planning a trip to HK in the future, don't worry, there is now a new longer runway.

Another thing to think about when you plan your trip is the weather. The typhoon season runs from May to November. These extraordinarily strong winds all have different names depending on what part of the world they occur in:

Typhoon in the Pacific;
Cyclone in South East Asia;
Hurricane in the North Atlantic;
Willy-willy in... can you guess?... Australia!

To be called one of the above names the wind must be at least 74 mph or 120 kph.

If your name is Patricia then you share the name of the most powerful storm of all time. Hurricane Patricia in 2015 set a world record with a top windspeed 215 mph! You would not want to be out in that! When you next listen to the weather forecast and the reporter says it's going to be windy, imagine what it would feel like to be in a typhoon or hurricane or even a willy-willy!

HK is where East meets West and brand shiny new meets with the ancient world. Like you, with all your technical stuff and knowledge, meeting your great-great-grandma! The new and very, very old all mixed up and living together; that was how HK seemed to me in 1993.

Our stay was brief, but enough time to experience the uncomfortable humidity and see the mess left by Typhoon Becky. Our taxi driver dodged fallen palm trees along the winding road up the Peak (a district of HK) where some friends of Barney's kindly let us sleep on their floor.

At an evening reception, we met business men and women who were kindly sponsoring us (they gave money, food and equipment) and we thanked them for their support. More photos and more press interviews.

Sensible members of the team went to bed, but Rupert and I thought, 'Come on, we might never get the chance to see HK again, let's go out.' The city was as busy by night as it was by day. Who could resist? Music boomed and fluorescent lights flashed. There were bars, restaurants, shops and street stalls selling everything you can imagine from noodles to fake Rolex watches and the latest 'Nike' trainers.

Spicy noodles at five o'clock in the morning was an interesting way to start the next leg of our journey.

You should try it; it certainly wakes you up!

We were on our way to Beijing, the capital of China, on a flight with 'Dragon Air.' That has to be the coolest name for an airline company ever.

CHAPTER 6

Bicycles, Fish Bladders And Slugs!

In Beijing we were greeted by Mr Guo, a short, rotund man, who was extremely smiley. He shook our hands enthusiastically, grinning and bowing as he welcomed us proudly to:

THE PEOPLE'S REPUBLIC OF CHINA.

Equipment, boxes, rucksacks and people squashed into minibuses whose drivers attempted to weave their way through the busy streets of Beijing. Never, not even when watching the Tour de France (a big bike race), had I seen so many people on bicycles: a sea of people on rickety old bikes. Somehow, they managed to keep moving and didn't crash or fall off, as taxis and yellow minibuses dodged around them. Bikes were in charge here and motorised vehicles had to behave. It didn't matter how much the drivers tooted their horns; the cyclists kept going. They were pedalling to work dressed mainly in dark trousers, skirts or gleaming white short-sleeved shirts, with the occasional gentleman in a dark blue **MAO SUIT**. Every now and then, a wide-brimmed straw hat to keep the sun off, bobbed pass our bus. Slowly they cycled, rang their bells and happily ignored all buses and taxi horns.

However, in the chaos, there did seem to be some order. Cyclists, taxi drivers, carts pulled by various animals, and buses, all obeyed smart policemen wearing long white gloves. They stood precariously high up on pedestals in the middle of the road, blew whistles and waved their arms. Whatever they were doing, it seemed to be working. Slowly, the traffic inched forward.

We arrived at a smart modern hotel. A long line of neatly dressed men in suits bowed and welcomed us to their hotel. (There's a lot of bowing in China as it's a gesture of respect.) That night, at a huge banquet held in our honour, we were welcomed, this time officially, by the highest dignitaries (very important people) in Beijing.

We were surprised by the attention. China was taking our expedition very seriously! It was a bit like a Royal Visit when the Queen, or one of her family, is invited to a far-off land and lavishly looked after. Obviously, I am not the Queen, and we are not members of the royal family, but our expedition did represent them.

The Chinese Government was determined to take care of us and treated us to a truly spectacular Chinese welcome. We were entertained with Chinese opera and music. This was accompanied by traditional dancing in colourful costumes, long speeches and, of course, extraordinary and unusual food.

Everything was filmed by Chinese Central Network (CCN) TV (similar to the BBC but in China), so we were all on our best behaviour.

Charles gave a speech, which Richard interpreted. It was greeted by very loud and enthusiastic clapping from everyone.

On a huge round table, I sat with smiling dignitaries and Mark interpreted. As the only woman at our table, and possibly at any table, I was quite a novelty. There was a lot of nodding and nervous laughter, mainly from me.

The feast started to arrive; Chinese women, beautifully dressed in brightly coloured silk gowns ceremoniously presented our table with huge plates of unusual looking food.

I wanted to know what we were eating and asked Mark.

I SHOULD NOT HAVE DONE THAT!

Mark said, 'FISH BLADDER.'

I wished I hadn't asked.

Next, he said, 'SEA SLUG.'

Grinning, he then added, 'And I am not joking!'

Eeeeeeekkkkk!

Have you ever been to a friend's house when their mum smiles and then gives you something to eat that everyone else seems to love but you really hate? Maybe BRUSSELS SPROUTS or broccoli. To be polite, you have to smile and eat them. Well, that was the situation I was facing.

All eyes were on me; everyone waited for me to take a bite. Mark encouraged me to pick up my chopsticks and get on with it, saying, 'They won't eat until you have tasted the food first.' He added, 'You need to look like you are enjoying it; your country is depending on you!' Nervously, I smiled, took a deep breath, and tucked into the unusual delicacies before me. I've never eaten fish bladder or sea slug before or since! They were tasty. It was just the names that made them sound horrid BLADDER, SLUG! Not the most appetising words. As more and more plates appeared with food that none of us recognised, I learnt to smile, eat, and not to ask questions.

China was giving us their most treasured delicacies and we were extremely honoured.

Later in the expedition we learnt that just as we found eating sea slugs and fish bladders unusual, the Chinese thought us odd drinking milk as grown-ups, saying with a smile and a laugh that we smelt like babies, and I don't think they meant nice clean ones that have just had a bath!!

CHAPTER 7

Gold Chairs and a Pot Noodle Mountain!

A meeting with the **British Ambassador** involved a rather serious discussion about what to do with our bodies should we, not to put too fine a point on it, 'kick the bucket', 'fizzle out'… Ok, I will say it – *DIE* in the desert! Anyway, let's not think about DYING in the desert. Let's think about food again.

Time to collect lots and lots of boxes of POT NOODLES, donated by a company in **Taiwan**. The noodle factory staff also wanted to pray daily for our safe passage across the desert. After the morning's discussion with the Ambassador, we needed all the help we could get!

At the airport, Rupert sat on a mountain of POT NOODLES – hundreds of boxes. 📷

Whatever else happened to us, we wouldn't go hungry.

As long as we had water to pour in the pot noodles! I haven't tried dry pot noodles, but I don't think they would be very nice.

A bumpy four-hour flight to **URUMCHI** followed. Every time I looked out of the window, I either saw mountains or deserts. We landed briefly in Urumchi, the capital of the area of China where the desert is.

Officials directed us to a large room with a thick red carpet. It looked a bit like a chamber in a palace (not that I've been in many palaces) but it's how I imagine it might be! Around the edge of the room stood large gold-coloured chairs; not the sort you have at home (unless you do live in a palace!) but more like thrones. Cameras flashed and film crews dashed around as important people from the area arrived to take their places on the ornate chairs. They welcomed us, wishing us good luck, and there was more hand-shaking, more bowing and, you've guessed it, more speeches!

The final plane to **KASHGAR** was old and ridiculously small. We squeezed in with all our kit (don't forget the noodles) and the Chinese film crew. No room for anyone else! We were given some odd-looking food in a box. This time, I remembered. Don't ask, just eat it.

After a bumpy landing that involved boxes of noodles rolling round the plane, I stepped onto the runway, feeling sick but relieved. It was very, very hot and something swirled around my feet...

SAND!

CHAPTER 8

Trucks and Awesome Camels!

Our support team was led by Barney in two special trucks with six wheels. (**Pinzgauer** all-terrain 6WD.) The company assured us they worked well in sand; we would see about that!

The first vehicle was driven by Barney and his old school pal, Francis. Francis worked in the City of London and had become bored of working in an office. His wife encouraged him to take a sabbatical (a long holiday from work). At team meetings, he was quiet, serious, dressed in a suit, and wore a long dark overcoat; he carried a black rolled umbrella (always) and a battered ancient briefcase. I remembered thinking when I first met him, that he looked like a tired James Bond. Barney and Francis worked as a team and tactfully pointed out when Charles' dreams/ideas were unrealistic or even dangerous. A bit like your parents saying to you, 'That's a great idea, but I am afraid it's not going to work!'

The second truck was owned and driven by **John and Anne Thomas**, a determined and formidable couple from the Welsh mountains. 📷 They had been on adventures all over the world. Resourceful and unfazed by pretty much any situation, their knowledge and expertise played a vital role in the expedition.

The vehicles were put in containers and shipped from Britain to the port of Karachi in Pakistan. Barney and his team collected them, signed some papers and then drove them to China.

I say it just like that, 'drove them to China.' This was no ordinary journey; it was over 1000 miles along an infamous road known as the **KARAKORAM HIGHWAY** passing through many border checkpoints, several mountain ranges, and crossing some of the most rugged and remote terrain in the world. Despite landslides, rock falls, unfriendly border guards, breakdowns, and upset stomachs, they managed to get to CHINA and... find us.

From a cloud of dust, with a roar of engines and lights on full beam, they appeared.

Smiles and hugs all round; finally, the team was together.

We packed up and continued towards the desert.

I bet you are thinking, 'Are they ever going to get to this desert?'

Our convoy of vehicles: two British trucks, Chinese buses, and lorries – oh, and don't forget the POT NOODLES – travelled along bumpy dusty roads lined by avenues of tall poplar trees. We passed strips of fertile land irrigated with water from the mountains. The bright green **paddy fields** were dotted with people working. In the distance, we could make out the beginning of small sand dunes.

ARE WE NEARLY THERE?

NOT QUITE!

Driving into the frontier town of **Markit**, the streets were lined with hundreds of people waving flags and cheering as they welcomed the desert explorers. We passed enormous heaps (taller than a double decker bus) of white fluffy stuff. Local people with large wicker baskets on their backs climbed rickety ladders to the top of the pile. They tipped out their loads of recently harvested **cotton**. Although Markit is on the edge of a desert it is one of the largest cotton producing areas in China. 📷

We attended more banquets and this time I had to dance with officials! Oh, how I wished I had paid more attention at school when Mr Lee, our PE teacher, tried to teach us the waltz. (That's a dance you might see on TV on a Saturday night, your gran probably watches it – *Strictly*! I also watch it now since my second cousin Rose Ayling Ellis was on it; she is awesome.)

More speeches and a local man described seeing snakes four metres long and lizards the size of crocodiles in the desert! (EEEEK) Many legends (stories usually based on SOME truth) are told about deserts. I REALLY hoped the old man's tales of giant snakes and lizards like dragons were not true!

The next morning, we were woken by the crackly sound of the tannoy system. It was a bit like a local radio station played to the whole town, whether they wanted to listen or not. Music and news blared out from battered old speakers dangling from posts that lined the streets. A lady came into my room, lit a candle and brought me hot water.

A bit odd, you might think, but there was no running water or electricity. The town might get some power, but it couldn't be relied upon.

After a breakfast of rice and **jasmine tea** we met our Chinese team mates.

Then the stars of our expedition arrived and made quite an entrance, bellowing and generally making a racket.

Big brown eyes with long lashes gazed upon us. We looked at them, and they looked at us. I felt nervous

Ok, let's be honest here. A bit, well – YES – frightened. These camels were HUGE! There were thirty Bactrian camels probably taller than you imagine, with two wobbly humps and thick woolly coats.

Lead by six **UYGHUR** camel-handlers, the camels strolled in, heads held high pretending not to be interested.

Imagine thirty camels arriving in your school playground. Exciting? Worrying? Fun?

Certainly, they would cause a commotion! The playground assistants would be hiding and your headteacher would be running out to see what on earth was going on!

I worked at my local zoo (Paignton) for a couple of days, but it had NOT prepared me for seeing thirty gigantic hairy Bactrian camels! They were much bigger than any you might see in a zoo, and so tall that if one walked into your bedroom, it would have to lower its head. Actually, its hump would touch the ceiling and, in fact, it wouldn't be able to get through your front door; so probably not a good idea to invite it in!

In charge of the camels was Esa Polta, an experienced camel farmer. He had wrinkled skin the colour of polished antique wood and a long wispy white beard that made him look like Gandalf from *The Hobbit* or Professor Dumbledore from *Harry Potter*... Instead of a wizard's hat, he wore a battered straw **PANAMA** from a football World Cup.

After some shouting, waving of sticks and grumpy sounds, mainly from the camels, they all sat down. 📷

📷
Go to website thecameldoc.com for a real life photo

CHAPTER 9

What's in the Bag?

On a large tarpaulin, I laid out my medical kit and thought hard about what to pack. I don't want you thinking this was the first time I'd considered what could go wrong. Over months of preparation, I tried to imagine all the things that could happen.

I talked to other expedition medics.

The truth is...

You have to be realistic.

Even if you are the world's greatest surgeon you're going to struggle at -20°C in a sandstorm.

I packed two medical kits, one for each team.

If you ever go on a family holiday or walking over the Scottish Highlands, your mum or dad, or maybe you, will take a small medical bag: stuff to deal with cuts, bumps, blisters and pain.

Like the medical bag your PE teacher rushes to get when you or one of your friends fall over. My expedition medical kit was similar to your school's or your mum's, just a bit bigger, and it included a few extra things. Like tablets to fight infections (antibiotics) and injections to help ease pain and treat allergic reactions (in case anyone was bitten by an unusual insect!) and lots of other stuff that hopefully I wouldn't need.

Rupert and Mark needed to test the radio equipment so they tried to make contact with Barney, who had driven to the edge of the desert.

'Hello, Bella, this is camel. Radio check, over.' There were lots of hissing and crackly sounds.

'Repeat, Hello, Bella, this is camel. Radio check, over.' Hiss, crackle, hiss, silence.

'Nothing heard, out,' said Rupert.

Not a good start to communications. The plan was to make radio contact with the support team every night at exactly the same time to tell them how we were getting on.

Barney would then send the information to head office in London.

Both teams had a call sign to identify them.

Barney's radio was BELLA.

Every expedition needs someone back at base who is organised, calm under pressure and generally amazing. This was Bella. She did everything from communicate with press, TV, the Royal Palace and our worried families, and she even managed to find a new engine for one of the trucks!

The crossing party's radio name was – can you guess?

CAMEL!

Everyone was busy doing something.

Keith, a tall young American from California, dashed around with lots of cameras around his neck. The team's official photographer, he was determined not to miss a thing.

As I quietly organised my medical stuff, I heard raised voices. Charles and Mr Guo were disagreeing!

Richard, an ex-**DIPLOMAT** who spoke fluent **MANDARIN**, tried to calm the situation.

Charles wanted all crossing team members to lay out their kit so he could check what everyone was packing, stating that the success of the expedition depended on the camels not being overloaded.

We laid out our kit, as did the Uyghurs, and most of the Chinese team did the same. Charles encouraged the now not-so-smiley Mr Guo to inspect the kit with him.

A tall, thin man from Beijing who said he was 'the professional photographer', refused to show Charles what was in his bags. The man stood with his hands on his hips and said, 'NO.' Mr Guo was agitated, eventually saying, 'It's against Chinese custom; he cannot be made to show us what is in his bags.'

Charles was angry and frustrated and looked as if he was going to explode. Richard quickly intervened, explaining to Charles some of the intricate details of Chinese etiquette about not **losing face**.

Wishing for no further upset, both sides agreed not to look in the bags.

Can you guess WHAT was in his bag?

You will find out, but not yet!

Next, we tested the petrol generator. What a racket, putt- putt-putting away as it belched out horrid smoke. The generator charged batteries and powered the satellite communication system. The satellite phone was the latest piece of high tech loaned to us by a company that wanted it tested in the harsh environment of a sandy desert. If it survived here, it could survive anywhere.

By late afternoon, everything was packed and the radio and satellite were working.

Rupert cheerfully reported, 'All systems go. We will now be able to tell the world when we are about to perish.' Strangely, we all laughed!

Perhaps you're thinking, 'Oh, well, if they get into trouble a helicopter can go and rescue them. Good idea.'

Our Chinese friends told us that a helicopter was available for emergencies... however, they had no fuel!

A helicopter with no aviation fuel is not very useful.

If we needed rescuing, it was up to Barney and his support team.

CHAPTER 10

Whirling Uyghur

(Just a reminder it's pronounced WE GAR.)

Charles called the British team together for a meeting, sort of like when your headteacher talks to you before important tests or a big sports match. He reminded us that we were representing our country and were privileged guests of the Uyghurs and the Chinese nation. Without their support there was NO expedition. Message received loud and clear: behave yourselves or else.

The town of Markit wanted to send us off in style. One more time of dressing up smartly – the boys in suits and ties and me in a dress. Our outfits seemed out of place as we walked along the dark, dusty streets. The camel-handlers and a few camels came with us as we were led through the eerily quiet town. A tall, imposing wall loomed out of the darkness. It was built of ancient, crumbling stone with two enormous green wooden doors.

Four men who had been leaning against the wall sprang to life and pushed with all their might. The doors creaked slowly open, revealing an arena lit only by flaming torches. Unsure of what to expect, we smiled at each other apprehensively. If in doubt, wave the Union Jack. We stepped forward and entered the arena. Deafened by cheering, the stadium was full of men, women, children, government officials, and soldiers in the uniform of the **People's Liberation Army**.

We were shown to a special area. The chairs were covered with beautiful fabrics and tapestry cushions: we sat and tried to take it all in. I really wish you could have seen it. Only now do

I realise how incredibly lucky we were. Sadly, the evening was not filmed.

A word of WARNING: If you plan an adventure and someone like the BBC says, 'Yes, we want to film the whole thing,' have a backup plan because they may let you down at the last minute. (The BBC wanted to film the whole crossing but pulled out two days before we left.) Sadly, this resulted in (YOU, MY MUM) everyone, missing out on seeing this historic event.

What we witnessed that evening was extraordinary hospitality and entertainment from a race and culture that is fast disappearing: the **UYGHUR PEOPLE**.

Music from a school band rang out into the hot night air.

Brightly coloured flags and costumes swirled around as the Uyghurs demonstrated their traditional dances. Mesmerised by the noise, colours, and fireworks, I had not realised that one of the village elders was asking me to dance.

'OH NO, do I have to do this?'

Charles nodded and Rupert and Mark roared with laughter. There was no escaping. I joined the whirling Uyghur to much amusement from my teammates. Their laughter soon stopped as they too were pulled out to dance. Our camels were not left out of the fun. They paraded with colourful garlands hung around their necks. As well as dancing, music, and fireworks… you've guessed it – more SPEECHES.

The Mayor of Markit announced that the following day would be a holiday to give everyone the chance to wave us off.

More cheering!

We really were taking part in something extraordinary.

CHAPTER 11

No Spitting. That's Not Very Nice!

After a night of partying, the public radio crackled and hissed into life. Scratchy violin music and booming voices announced the departure of the Chinese, Uyghur and British heroes.

Groan! Suddenly I remembered 'BRITISH HEROES'. Help! I am one of them! Come on, get up! It's not a dream or a nightmare, it's actually happening!

In the compound outside, the Uyghur camel-handlers were busy feeding the camels. It would be their last proper meal for many weeks. Greedily, they ate and drank as much as they could; camels, you will learn, are good at eating. This was the final walk towards the edge of the desert.

You may be thinking: ARE WE NEARLY THERE YET?

Almost, but not quite!

The British and Chinese support vehicles were jammed full of equipment, food and people.

Plus, VERY IMPORTANT: Loading camels.

On that first morning, we watched and studied the camel-handlers. Hired by Charles, we were told these men were experts at looking after camels.

We had to learn from them, and quickly.

Sounds easy?

How do you get on packing your school bag, especially on a day when you have sports?

I expect it involves a fair amount of stress, running around shouting, 'I can only find one hockey sock, where are my football boots, and who's moved my homework?'

Imagine packing forty large camel sacks every day, sometimes in the dark or a sandstorm!

Can you believe that camels don't really want to carry a heavy load or any load for that matter? What a fuss they made dashing about, bellowing, and yes – that thing you've probably heard about – SPITTING!

Stand back – and keep your wits about you.

You do not want to be covered in foul-smelling half- digested camel food! That radio programme I was on all those months ago came into my head. Remember how everyone laughed when I said, 'I hope to come back and tell you that NOT ALL CAMELS ARE BAD!'

Looking around, I wasn't so sure about that now!

What a commotion! Surely it wasn't going to be like this every morning. We had to hope we learnt quickly and the camels started liking us!

The camels were fitted with soft padded saddles, purchased from a local bazaar. A good sale for someone. I can't imagine they often sold thirty in one go!

Twenty camels carried large double camel sacks. Let me try to explain about these sacks. Like me, you probably haven't seen many camel bags. Imagine two huge square pockets of strong woven fabric stitched together at the top, thrown over the saddle, then secured in place with ropes. (That's how a camel sack works.) You must balance out the load, otherwise the camel will be lopsided and even more unhappy! They need roughly the same weight on each side. Unlucky camels got two bags of **split grain** (camel food): the heaviest load. Others carried equipment and supplies. Ten carried the new, shiny, oblong metal water containers that had been stacked in the corner of the compound. Other than counting the water containers, we had not paid much attention to them. Later this proved to be a BIG, no – a HUGE MISTAKE!

A camel carried one tin on each side. When full, the container holds eighty litres of water. That's about the same as 240 cans of lemonade – on each side!!

The camel-handlers shout a command that sounded like, 'JUGGER'; apparently it means 'stand up'.

Someone needed to tell the camels that.

They remained seated, chewing, looking bored and gazing at us, probably thinking, 'These guys have got NO CHANCE!' Eventually, with some encouragement, they stood up. Two ropes were thrown underneath them and then they sat back down and the containers were secured into position.

That's how you load a camel. SIMPLE!

Well, let me tell you, it didn't look simple, and the camels were not that enthusiastic about it either!

CHAPTER 12

Fire Crackers and Camel Stamps

Hooray! I packed my dress and smart shoes, giving them to the support team for safe keeping. I was much happier wearing expedition gear: my walking boots (as worn on Dartmoor) and trusty Aussie bush hat.

Some of the camel-handlers' children came to wave their dads and grandads off.

They smiled when we gave them expedition badges but were even more excited to be given packets of biscuits. 📷 They had certainly never had British biscuits before.

Flags were unfurled and attached to poles. A huge red banner stretched across the road in front of us saying,

'Here's the JOINT BRITISH, CHINESE EXPEDITION which will attempt to cross the Taklamakan Desert!'

Note the word 'ATTEMPT.'

Although there was excitement about our 'attempt', there was little confidence amongst the locals that we would succeed!

Chinese people love fire crackers and will set them off at any opportunity. Fireworks are thought to have been discovered in China about 2000 years ago when a cook accidentally mixed charcoal, sulphur and saltpetre... BOOOM! (Don't try this recipe if you go on the *Great British Bake Off*!!) Firecrackers popped and danced around us, creating clouds of blue grey smoke. Fortunately, the camels had seen fireworks before and hardly blinked.

Divided up into camel trains (which is just a long line of camels all tied together), groups of five or six were led out onto the sandy main street of Markit. We followed them down the dusty road, lined with people cheering and waving flags. An enthusiastic school band with dented trumpets serenaded us as we slowly but surely walked towards the desert. 📷 Along the route, we were directed into a large parade ground for yet more entertainment and, you've guessed it, more SPEECHES!

Children, like you and your friends, dressed in colourful uniforms, danced, smiled and waved flags. Perfectly in step, they must have practised for many weeks 📷 I felt incredibly lucky to be taking part in a world first, even if it was an 'attempt!'

On an old wooden stage, we were presented with traditional Uyghur costumes. 📷 The men were wrapped in **chapans**: long dark coats tied in the middle by a broad band of material. I was dressed in a silk gown with a bright geometric pattern. On our heads were placed the doppa a square or round skull cap, usually black or white with colourful embroidery; as the only girl I was given a special one that was purple and gold.

Luckily, everything could be worn over the top of our clothes, otherwise it might have been embarrassing, changing in front of all those people.

I think you can see that we looked a bit awkward, especially Rupert.

We just wanted to get to the desert!

As I am sure you do too!

Charles was presented with beautiful handmade wooden musical instruments: a gift from the Uyghur people of Markit and the Xinjiang region.

As if the dressing up and all that dancing wasn't enough, now we were asked to sign our names on hundreds – and I do mean hundreds – of envelopes. Have you seen those special ones that commemorate something important like the Olympics or the Queen's Jubilee?

A special camel stamp and first day cover had been released across China to celebrate the attempted crossing. 📷 There's that word again – 'ATTEMPT!'

They insisted we signed them before we left. Perhaps if we went missing in the desert, the first day covers with our autographs might be worth a lot of money. Especially if they sold them to our mums!

Some kind Uyghur women spoke to me. 📷 They were crying; the stories of people disappearing in the desert were real to these women. They believed we were going to a certain death and begged me not to go.

I had not prepared myself for this sort of thing happening.

Was I worried? Honestly, not really, but then I had no idea what the desert had in store for us. I should have been worried; those women knew all about the desert and its fearsome reputation. You wouldn't catch them wandering off into the sand dunes.

I held their hands, smiled and thanked them for their concern, assuring them I would be fine. (My fingers were crossed!)

The ceremony dramatically finished with the release of white doves and blessings from local **Imams**, entrusting Allah to guide us through the desert, whose cheery names include, in case you've forgotten:

1. The Desert of Death!

2. The Desert of No Return!

We were going to need all the help we could get!

Back on the road, we inched closer to the desert. As we approached the edge of Markit, the crowds disappeared and the eerie peace of the Taklamakan descended upon us.

ARE WE THERE YET?

YES!

CHAPTER 13

Filling Water Containers and A Maths Test!

We stopped at the edge of the desert and made camp for the first night in the sand dunes. 📷

There was still quite a crowd following us: the support teams and their vehicles, Uyghur camel-handlers' families, film crews and press. Also, some curious locals, wondering what on earth we were all up to.

Oh, and don't forget thirty camels strolling around munching on pieces of very dry bush. They appeared happier than anyone else; this after all, was their world. Unlike us, they are designed to be in the desert. The camel-handlers were also glad to be away from the crowds and the bureaucracy of town life. So, the Uyghurs and camels were happy, but the rest of us were anxious, disorganised and not looking very cheerful.

An old blue water truck slowly spluttered its way to the edge of our encampment. This was how we filled the water containers. (NO TAPS OUT HERE!)

Remember those shiny new tins in the compound that we counted, but never really took much notice of? We began to fill each of the twenty containers with water for the FIRST time.

Can you guess what happened?

Six of them LEAKED, and I don't mean a little drip!

Precious water spurted out from the corners of the tins, disappearing into the hot sand. 📷

NOT a good start to our expedition.

Charles was angry with himself for not checking the containers before. Later, he was annoyed with **Zhang**, the Chinese second-in-command and interpreter, who was sent to the local bazaars to get the holes fixed. Instead, he returned with large plastic bottles that also leaked from around the lids. No time to waste, we cut up material and plastic sheets and tried to improve the seal; it wasn't brilliant, but it helped.

Charles and Barney anxiously calculated how much water we were now able to carry. We needed a certain amount to survive until the first resupply.

Let me try to explain how Charles planned the expedition. The Taklamakan desert is roughly 1000 miles across (IF you walked in a straight line!) from West to East.

The support team travelled on the Southern Silk Road and mirrored our journey. At the start of the crossing, they were just a few miles from us. After about a week, we were well into the desert and the support team was several hundred miles away.

The expedition was divided up into five phases. At the end of a phase, the support team drove as far as they could into the desert to resupply us with food and, most importantly, water! Some of the resupply points were in tiny desert settlements. According to local information, there was a good chance of finding water in the desert to 'water the camels.' That's an odd expression 'water the camels' – it doesn't mean you fill up a watering can and tip it over the camels (although they might have liked that), it means: give them water to drink!

Charles didn't talk much about our chances of finding water. The truth was, if we didn't find water for the camels, we were all in BIG trouble!

Looking around at the vast sandy expanse, it didn't seem obvious how or where the water would be found.

Camels get moisture from things they eat, even from thorny desert plants like **tamarisk**. These bushes were found in some areas where there was a tiny bit of moisture. You might see these dry woody plants at the seaside, hard to imagine getting any water out of them.

Camels can survive three to five days without a drink but, rather like you and me, they prefer water every day.

We calculated our water requirements again and again.

You know when you have a maths lesson at school, and you think to yourself, when will I ever need to use this?

If you go on a trip to a desert, working out how much water each person needs is vital.

You need to be absolutely sure you've calculated correctly. 8/10 won't do, this is a gold star, 10/10 maths test.

Charles paced around the desert scratching his head and looking worried. 'Each person needs five litres a day; that's two litres for drinking, one litre spare for emergency, plus two litres for communal cooking.'

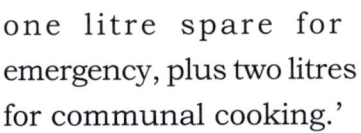

Charles admitted quietly to us that his calculations were tight. They didn't allow for much wastage from drips, spillage and evaporation.

When the silver tins, plus some odd plastic bottles, were full, we had around 1800 litres of precious drinking water. 'Hopefully,' said Charles, 'that will get us to the first resupply!'

'HOPEFULLY!'

That's another one of those words like

ATTEMPT

I don't like those words; they are not very encouraging!

CHAPTER 14

Last Letter Home

On the edge of the desert while their parents prepared a feast the camel-handler's children played, proudly wearing the badges we had given them: a Union Jack with a camel and the initials **CCCC (Camel Crossing for Children's Cancer)**. 📷 Spread upon the desert floor was a giant blue tarpaulin laden with food. Like a huge picnic but no sandwiches or sausage rolls in sight. The Uyghur families invited us to sit around the edge. We sat together. Prayers of thanks were said, before the Uyghurs kindly shared their food. The 'feast' included watermelons, grapes, mutton, goat and Uyghur naan (a local bread). The naan we nicknamed 'Sven Hedin bread rolls', and you will find out why near the end of the book. 📷

The satellite phone was working so we were allowed one very short call home. It's a tough one – you're a long way from home and about to do something dangerous. You want to speak to your family but, at the same time, you don't want to hear that something is wrong at home, as you won't be able to help.

I spent most of the call to my mother who had not been expecting my call saying, 'YES, IT'S ME' and 'Yes, I am in China on the edge of the desert!' Apparently, I sounded as if I was just down the road! It was good to hear her voice and reassuring to know the phone worked!

I busied myself ensuring the medical kit was ready. Using a big red felt pen, I put a large cross on one of the camel sacks and placed my red tool box inside: the main medical kit.

I carried a small amount of emergency supplies in my **day sack**.

Plus, I loaded up my waistcoat, stashing odd pills, potions and plasters in various pockets.

It's like one of those fishing jackets with lots of very useful pockets to carry all sorts of things, including EMERGENCY SWEETS!

Although nervous, I was ready; I just wanted to get started.

We sat quietly around the campfire, lost in our own thoughts. Heads down, we wrote diaries and letters home.

In the morning the letters were sealed up and solemnly handed over to Barney. The instructions were written in capitals across the envelope:

ONLY TO BE OPENED IN THE EVENT OF MY DEATH.

Sounds serious, and it was; what do you write in a letter that MIGHT be your last words home?

No need for a long essay, I wrote something like;

EDGE OF TAKLAMAKAN DESERT, CHINA
23rd September 1993

I'm really sorry,
please don't be sad.
I've always tried to follow my
dreams but this one seems
to have gone a bit wrong.
If you are reading this,
hold a party that's a CELEBRATION
of my life.
I've been very lucky, done a lot
of INCREDIBLE things, and had
a huge amount of Fun
(although not so lucky on this
occasion, ha ha)

Thankyou to the most
AMAZING and SUPPORTIVE
family and friends...
Get the champagne out!
Look at the photos of the amazing
adventures I have had.
If you do remember me, please
do so with a smile ☺
and GFI (go for it!)
...live life to the full!

— Carolyn x

Despite our joking and bravado, we were taking the desert and its reputation very seriously.

The Chinese Central Television (CCTV) filmed our final farewells. Mr Guo represented the Chinese team. He spoke of Chinese heroes and bravery. The Uyghurs spoke quietly, uncomfortable in front of the camera; they showed great respect for the desert. Living on its edge, they knew more than we did about the challenges ahead.

Keith, the American, was filmed next and became upset during his interview. Charles struggled, fighting back tears as he spoke about his wife and three young sons.

The frightening reality of what we were about to 'ATTEMPT' had suddenly dawned on us.

That evening, for the first time, the whole crossing party slept together under the desert stars.

Six Uyghur camel-handlers,
Four Chinese,
Four British,
One American,
Thirty camels.

CHAPTER 15

Union Jack Upside Down!
BP Gets Heat Stroke

D day (desert day)!

Tying on the bulging camel sacks and full water containers was difficult. One camel was spooked; he didn't like something dangling down his leg.

AAAAGH! Did something touch my leg??!

He broke free from the camel train and ran off bellowing and bucking into the dunes.

During his antics, he dislodged his load – no doubt part of his plan. A water container landed heavily on the desert floor, split open, and eighty litres of water vanished into the hot sand. One day's supply of water gone in an instant.

It was a chaotic scene with camels and people running around; not the most promising start.

Things could only get better!

Have you ever volunteered for something like doing a solo in the school choir or being the goalkeeper for the hockey team and then on the day thought how on earth did I get myself into this and WHY?

Well, that was exactly what I was thinking as I watched camels running off into the desert with people chasing them! This wasn't the first time I'd got myself into a tricky situation, I constantly seemed to volunteer or somehow get involved with unusual and often dangerous things including parachuting, mountaineering, caving, being winched up a very tall ships mast in a storm because no one else would do it, to going to war and then speaking to hundreds of very important people about it when we got home! I remember thinking as I jumped out of a plane that this was not the most sensible thing

I had done, but you are going to have to do it... because you have told people you are doing it!!! That was the same feeling as we entered the desert, you have to do it because you've been banging on about it for over a year, so get out there and give it your best shot.

All team leaders were talking and emotions were running high. Richard and Mark desperately tried to interpret several different languages.

The national flags were up and blowing in the wind. In the rush to get going, the Union Jack was flying upside down!

We decided to leave it like that. 📷 You might not know, but a Union Jack upside down is an international sign of emergency or distress! Rupert joked that we might need that in the next few weeks!

Charles was determined to get moving
'NO MORE WAITING,
No more trying to sort things out,
No more interviews,
No more SPEECHES!!

WE ARE HEADING INTO THE DESERT AT 12.30 today, the 23rd of September.'

It was autumn going into winter. The longer we left it, the worse the weather would be. You might be thinking, odd they left at the hottest time of day, and you would be right.

It was HOT, HOT, HOT. Camera crews ran ahead of us, as first Rupert, with his compass-bearing set, walked purposefully out into the dunes, followed by Charles and Mr Guo.

A snaking line of thirty heavily laden camels, divided up into five camel trains, slowly followed. Camels will not rush for anyone. They have their own pace and that is the speed they will walk at. People cheered and applauded, firecrackers popped and jumped around the sand dunes, cameras clicked, and team members hugged each other. Barney walked with us for a few miles into the desert.

We laughed and joked, but I sensed anxiety in his voice. He had a huge responsibility if things went wrong; our lives depended on him. I was confident that if there was a way to save us Barney would find it.

In some ways, the crossing team had the easy bit; we just kept walking while the support team watched, waited and monitored our progress, offering help, guidance and encouragement just at the right time. We were like the star strikers of a football team and the support team were cheering us on. Charles was the captain and Barney was our manager.

I wasn't going to mention this, but as we set off into the desert, not only did we leave footprints in the sand, we also left a rather ominous, drip, drip, drip of H2O. It's embarrassing to admit that we entered a desert called 'the Desert of Death' LEAKING WATER! I think it's very important I tell you the truth; we all make mistakes and even explorers get things wrong, but not all admit it. This was our first mistake but unfortunately not our last!

On the first afternoon in the desert, the smallest of the Uyghurs, Abdul Rasheed, collapsed with heat stroke. He was only wearing his thin Muslim skullcap and the temperature was 40°C. It was hot, hot, hot like being a sausage in a very hot dry frying pan, if you can imagine that... not much fun. Luckily a light cooling breeze made life a little more bearable. Rupert and Charles alerted me to the stumbling camel-handler. I sat him down, cooled him, and made him drink lots of special water to which I had added medicine (a salt and sugar mixture).

Abdul needed to drink more and wear a hat that protected him from the sun. He was given a green British petroleum sponsor's hat, which he wore over his Muslim cap.

He became affectionately known as BP.

Rupert and I wore Australian wide-brimmed cattle ranchers' hats, Charles wore a military jungle hat, Richard a Barring's sponsor's hat and Keith wore an American baseball cap.

The Uyghurs and Chinese wore a variety of different sponsors' caps. I reminded everyone how important it was to drink lots, to create some shade by wearing hats, and to use sunscreen. No one took any notice!

The Chinese and The Uyghurs were not going to listen to a WOMAN! (Not yet anyway!)

Annoyed, I asked Charles to give the message again.

The first night sleeping out in the desert was a bit odd to say the least. We had not yet established any rules or routines. The Uyghurs slept near the camels, the Chinese slept together near the fire and Charles, Rupert, Richard and I put our sleeping bags near each other. There was no shower or wash before bed, although I did brush my teeth. We didn't use tents it was just easier to lie on the sand. Snuggled up in my sleeping bag, I gazed at the stars trying to get to sleep and started hearing an odd sound. Then I remembered the ghost stories told by local people about demons and strange happenings in the desert. Obviously, I didn't believe such stories but I was finding it hard to ignore the wailing sounds. I pulled my sleeping bag over my head, but could still hear it. Could anyone else hear it? Now I was getting scared what was the weird wailing sound, like someone in pain? Enough was enough I sat bolt upright in my sleeping bag and in a loud voice said, 'Can anyone else hear that noise?'

Charles shot up and said 'Thank goodness you can hear it too' Everyone else seemed to be asleep, so together Charles and I set off to investigate. We walked towards the strange sound. We were relieved to discover that it was in fact one the Uyghurs. A camel had gone missing and Kirim had gone to find it and as he walked back to camp, he started... singing... well that's what he called it!

We laughed and went back to our sleeping bags.

Phew... no ghosts!

CHAPTER 16

Compass Bearings and 'Miss, Can I Go to the Toilet?'

I think you need more information about the desert and some of the routines we established.

The Taklamakan Desert is shaped like a giant egg lying on its side. Charles wanted to walk in a straight line across the middle from West to East, left to right across the egg, I mean the Earth! That's about the equivalent distance of the whole length of Great Britain, with no roads, no towns, no trees just SAND!

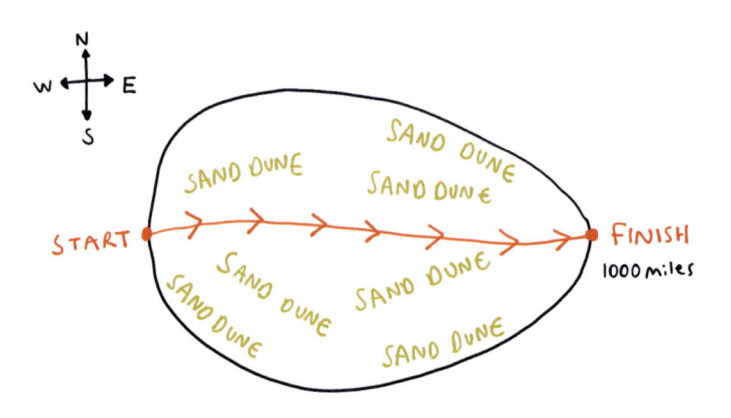

Crossing team members were all given a **Silva expedition compass**. Each morning, Charles announced the compass bearing – the direction for that day. Everyone then set their compass. It's simple – you just turn the dial. If you became separated from the main group, it was important you knew the line to follow. Even though we made a lot of noise as we walked along, sound and footprints disappeared quickly in the desert.

You are probably thinking, why on earth would you leave your friends and run the risk of getting separated from the team?

WHY did we nip off behind a sand dune?

Yep, you've guessed it: a call of nature.

'MISS, CAN I GO TO THE TOILET?'

There are no toilets in the desert. I think you know that.

So, here's what you do…

Tell a pal you are dashing to the dune!

Leave the camel train and disappear behind a sand dune. It's very private and quiet, a pleasant place to do your thing! However, when you have finished and come out from behind the dune… where has everyone gone? HELP! I am all alone and lost in this giant desert!

DON'T PANIC. Get your compass out of your pocket and off you go. Fingers crossed you find your friends. Although this process definitely works, personally, I was not keen to test it out, preferring when possible to visit the dunes during various breaks.

The camel-handlers were getting to know the camels' characters and had divided them up into groups. Initially, this was a random choice of who was where, when they started roping them together. If a camel made a fuss – Camel Number 8 for instance, it was left until the end of loading, when it might be lucky and not need to carry anything. Each day, we consumed food and water, lightening the loads and reducing the amount that needed transporting.

All domestic (working) camels are branded; a hot iron number is burnt into the thick hair on their hind legs. I am told it doesn't hurt (!). They do have names, but many look similar; the numbers helped farmers and us to identify them more easily.

Charles constantly reminded us how important it was that we work together and establish a routine. He wanted us to be ready to move by 09.30 every day. Loading in the mornings took at least two hours. We were still learning the delicate and sometimes hazardous task. Camels have a reputation of not always being the most cooperative creatures, especially in the morning. Does that sound like anyone you know? Your big brother maybe, or, thinking about it, could it be you?

It's definitely me, although I have learnt not to kick and spray my breakfast over everyone. This was the delight that awaited you if you were not careful with your camels in the morning!

Rupert led the expedition out, walking on the compass bearing decided by Charles; he tried to find the easiest way through the sand dunes but maintaining the correct direction. Going the right way is always a good idea!

Perhaps you've heard stories of people going round in circles in deserts and getting lost. It's easy to do because everything looks the same. Keeping to the correct route required constant checking as we twisted and turned our way through the dunes. As well as the hand-held compass, we also referred to a satnav (**satellite**

navigation GPS). 📷 It accurately measured how far we had travelled that day across the desert/Earth (egg!) and how far we still had to go until the very end! As the device scrolls through its distances, we covered up the last figure.

No one wants to know how many hundreds and hundreds of miles until the end. Darn it, I've seen it... 980!

That's 980 miles in a straight line until the end of the desert!!!!

Of course, we will not be walking in a straight line, so it would be well over 1000 miles. Up, down and around mile after mile of sand dunes!!!

Make sure the next time you look at the sat nav, you don't look at the last number, it's just too depressing!

CHAPTER 17

How to Find Water in a Desert

Each camel train was led by an Uyghur camel-handler. A second person walked at the back and another team member at the side, waving a big stick and shouting 'Char, char!', which means something like, 'Come on, you can do this.' Usually, that was enough to keep them moving. Occasionally, they needed stronger encouragement, but only when absolutely necessary. For example, a camel might stop on a high dune. This was dangerous and put everyone at risk. You must keep the camels moving to avoid them tumbling down, and ending up in a tangled mess at the bottom of a **sand mountain**.

If a camel ran out of steam on the slopes of a treacherously high dune, a quick tap on their rear helped them find a little more energy.

We pulled on the lead rope and pushed them from behind, leaning our shoulders into their hind quarters, a bit like being in a rather tricky rugby scrum.

We pushed and pushed... up and over the dunes, walking for between seven and nine hours every day. 📷 We did have breaks – half an hour for lunch and various other unplanned stops when camel sacks fell off and had to be reloaded.

Towards the end of every day, Rupert, Charles, and the lead camel-handler, Esa Polta, started looking for somewhere to stop for the night. Our overnight camp didn't look like a welcoming **oasis**. There was no luscious vegetation or palm trees and no waterhole or indeed anyone selling ice cream! It also wasn't like a campsite in Devon or Cornwall you might stay in with your parents. Our camp was just SAND DUNES with perhaps the odd tamarisk bush where, fingers crossed, we might find water! We looked in the valleys between the dunes for dry wispy **reeds** and a white salty crust on top of the sand. I agree, it doesn't sound that promising. However, it indicated that if we were lucky, we might find water deep under the sand. There was no actual water on the surface, but by digging down, sometimes as deep as two to three metres (imagine the two tallest teachers in school standing on top of each other that's how deep we had to dig), a salty water known as **brackish water** appeared.

A bit like if you dig a hole in the sand at the beach, water starts to seep into the bottom, then if you're not careful the sides collapse in! We needed to be careful!

Water slowly seeped into the deep hole. When there was enough, buckets were filled and hauled to the surface.

One of the camel-handlers tasted the water and shouted, 'sweet,' meaning good for camels to drink, or 'bad,' too salty and not good for humans or camels. 📷 Usually, the water was ok for camels and for cooking. Unlike humans, camels actually need lots of salt in their diet to stay healthy. We tried every day to find water for our camels to drink, we didn't always succeed.

At the beginning of the expedition, it was hot, hot, hot. When digging for water, some team members took off their boots. Tired, sore feet enjoyed the icy sensation of the waterlogged sand as we squished and sloshed around, chatting and laughing about the day's adventures.

Rupert always led the Uyghur's digging as they tried to find water. He was strong, possessed enormous energy, and was able to keep going, laughing and talking for many hours until water was found. Although they spoke different languages, the camel-handlers liked Rupert very much.

They looked up to him (quite literally as he was very tall and they were quite short), and they admired his energy, fortitude and friendly approach to life. They took turns to dig, watching as the hole got deeper and deeper and filled with water. The Uyghurs gave Rupert the nickname Luotuo (camel). They smiled and said, 'He is strong and eats as much as a camel.' Which was true!

Whenever the Uyghurs called Rupert Luotuo, which was most days, they laughed and smiled at him.

Each night we stopped just before the sun went down. Sadly, none of us ever managed to take a photo of the spectacular sunsets. Too busy unloading camels.

We never tied up or **hobbled** the camels. They are bright creatures and knew to stay close to us because we had all the food and water.

They were led into camp,

Sat down,

Untied,

Unloaded,

Stood up, and moved away.

This was the unchanging daily routine.

The camel sacks were left in little heaps all over the desert ready for the next morning, when we led the camels back in between the cans or sacks and reloaded. 📷

Free of their loads, the camels wandered around, sometimes peering down into the waterhole, to see how we were getting on.

If they were lucky half of them had a drink before midnight, and the others received their buckets just before dawn. This was a time of great excitement as they jostled and pushed each other, trying to be the first in line to get the buckets of icy cold water.

Although extremely hot during the day at night the desert was freezing. Sand gets really hot during the day but when the sun goes down all the heat from the sand disappears into the air and the temperature quickly drops.

CHAPTER 18

Nightly Routines and Camel Kicks!

With military precision, Rupert attempted to make radio contact with the support team every night. Laying the antenna out across the dunes, he sat on the sand twiddling dials and speaking – well, actually more like shouting, into the receiver, 'Hello, Bella, this is Camel. Do you receive me? Over.' He was not always able to make contact. Sometimes there was interference on the airwaves. When he did get through, it made us very happy. We gave our teammates reports on weather, health of the team, the camels and, most importantly, where we were and how far we had travelled across the desert that day.

Charles studied his maps, wrote up his diary, spoke to the support team, and generally ensured everyone was OK. My main job was to set up a treatment area – a sort of open-air clinic or mini-A&E/Casualty for all team members. I pulled my medicine box with the big red cross from the camel sack, laid out my roll mat, and awaited customers! Any member of the crossing team feeling unwell or injured could see me. I did my best to fix the problem with tablets, plasters, and general advice. At the beginning of the expedition, several team members had trouble with their feet. Crazily, some had NEW BOOTS, putting them on for the first time on the edge of the desert!

Just saying: a girl didn't make that mistake!

Remember, I made sure my boots were comfy by wearing them running over the moors! The combination of new boots, sand, heat and more walking than most were used to, resulted in some spectacular blisters. I must admit, I rather enjoyed popping, squeezing and taping up my teammates' feet. Although I did insist they washed them in the waterhole or at least gave them some air before waving them under my nose!

Keith's feet were covered in giant blisters.

The youngest of us, with no military experience, he was struggling. I patched him up as best as I could. 📷

At the end of my clinics, I gave Charles a briefing on team fitness and wellbeing. I was worried about Keith's feet. I shared my concerns with Charles.

Keith agreed to leave the crossing party at the first resupply to allow his feet chance to heal and give him the opportunity to photograph the support team's journey along the Southern Silk Road.

My clinics were daily events. I saw everything from blisters to sunstroke, diarrhoea, and lots and lots of bumps and bruises from camel kicks.

Luckily camels' huge feet (size of a dinner plate) have soft cushioned pads. Although they can kick – and they will – IN ALL DIRECTIONS, it might knock you over but usually won't break any bones! Quickly, we learnt the distance a camel kick could reach, which is considerably further than you might think! They kick out, and then, just when you are thinking, wooooooow that was close, they find a little extra stretch, and boom, contact is made and over you go AGAIN!!

Camels, just like humans, have different personalities; some are nice and calm and others are grumpy and prone to lash out at any opportunity.

WARNING: IF you ever need to pass a grumpy camel, do so with great care and it's probably best to approach from the head end!

CHAPTER 19

Spies, Secret Agents and Camel Breakfast

The Chinese team were not keen on eating our food (what's wrong with baked beans?) preferring to eat traditional Chinese food. They took charge of evening meals, as we were not fussy, happy eating anything – even fish bladder and SEA SLUGS!!! Luckily, they didn't have any more of those.

Most nights it was difficult to know what we were eating. As you know, I had learnt that it was best not to ask!

We were always hungry and the food tasted good, so we wolfed it down, no questions asked. If you adore Chinese takeaway **Sichuan** style (spicy) this is the trip for you, because you are going to eat it every single day!

The Chinese photographer, Qui (remember? He's the guy that wouldn't let Charles look in his bag) had an odd nightly routine.

He staggered across the sand dragging one of his big bags, disappeared, or so he thought, behind a large dune.

A long bendy pole went up into the night sky.

'As I suspected,' shouted Charles, 'he has a radio to keep in touch with officials in Beijing. He's a SPY, spying on us because they think we are spies!'

Charles, Rupert, Richard and I laughed. But we were annoyed that the camels were being made to carry unnecessary things. We were, after all, NOT SPIES!

As the days went by, Charles and Richard managed to persuade Qui to get more involved with team activities. He helped with some of the camp chores, albeit reluctantly and never with a smile. He remained suspicious of us and our motives for being in the desert, believing we were secret agents up to no good!

The Uyghur people are **Muslims** and for cultural and religious reasons they camped in a slightly different area from the main group. They quickly established which direction **Makkah** (in English **Mecca**) was, so they could conduct their regular prayers by turning to face the holy city. Quietly and without fuss, they got on with things.

The camels preferred to be near the Uyghurs. It was what they were used to. So, although not tethered, they generally stayed close.

The mornings were always entertaining with all sorts of antics from people and camels.

The camels had breakfast early, which meant they were **chewing the cud** as we attempted to load them.

As **pseudoruminants** with three stomachs, camels regurgitate their breakfast and chew it several times to get all the goodness and moisture out of it… lovely!

LOOK OUT if you load them without care, if the ropes are too tight or they are just grumpy and don't feel like carrying anything that day.

If you have annoyed them, they will let you know and, to demonstrate their displeasure, our beloved camels sprayed foul-smelling half-digested breakfast at unlucky people standing near them. YUCK!

As we go along through this adventure, you will learn that people who have been in the army like to give everything a nickname. We referred to this morning delight as being 'Hit by **CAMEL BREAKFAST**'!

For whatever reason, poor Rupert was covered in 'camel breakfast' more often than anyone else. 📷 For a close-up if you dare!

This is a good time to remind you that in a desert you only have water for drinking.

NO WATER FOR WASHING!

For those of you who, one day, might be unlucky enough to be 'hit by camel breakfast' here's Rupert telling you what to do.

'The trick for dealing with camel breakfast on your clothes is let it dry out and then take your penknife and scrape it off.'

I think you will agree that sounds horrid!

It also doesn't work. In the heat of the midday sun, Rupert walked alone!

Dried-on camel breakfast had a certain aroma (WHIFF!).

CHAPTER 20

What Time Is It?

Do you wear a watch or look at your phone for the time? Whatever you do, we live by the clock. We get up at a certain time, with some encouragement, and we go to school or work, hopefully arriving on time. We have routines that we sometimes need to be reminded of, and usually by a very shouty and stressy parent!

BRUSH YOUR TEETH!

SHOES!

SCHOOL BAG!

COAT!

WHOOPS, you've forgotten your HOMEWORK. Again!

Our lives are controlled by time, and it was no different in the desert. Charles, Rupert, Richard, Keith and I lived by our watches, however the Uyghurs and Chinese had different ideas, as you will see later.

Only one of our watches had an alarm function. Thank goodness for Rupert's watch, otherwise I am not sure how we would have woken up each morning. At night, the watch was handed over to the person whose turn it was to wake up first. We took it in turns. When I say *we*, I mean the British team. No one else was prepared to move before they absolutely had to.

Believe it or not, I liked doing the early morning wake up. I enjoyed the peace and being busy. I am bit odd; I like routines! Come with me now as I try to explain an early morning start. You will need your big puffy coat, hat, gloves, and headtorch; it's dark and cold.

1. The first thing to do is get the fire going.

You are probably thinking, how can you have a fire in a desert? Where does the wood come from? Good question.

Luckily for us, many thousands of years ago the desert didn't exist. Instead, there was a big lake surrounded by a forest. The tops of old trees poked up through the sand. As we walked along, if we spotted some wood, we picked it up and the camels carried it. A bright, warming fire always cheered everyone up. The wood, as you might expect, was dry and burnt really well. It's about 05.30. I am kneeling in the sand with my face very close to the fire. There is faint glow. I gently put on some small twigs (**kindling**).

Take a deep breath. You need to blow softly for a long time. There is something magical about blowing on glowing embers and watching a fire suddenly burst into life. Immediately, your face lights up and you smile and feel the warmth. The fire crackles and the area around lights up. If you're not careful, you can find yourself staring into the fire; you go into sort of a trance, gazing at the flames and not wanting to leave them.

BUT there's NO time to waste. You've got jobs to do.

Here's a secret to help your morning routine go well.

The night before, as you head off to your sleeping bag, make sure the fire is stocked up with wood and burning well. Collect some small sticks ready for action in the morning. Here's the secret... take the kindling with you to bed. I know it sounds odd, BUT if you leave it by the fire someone will burn it. Then, in the morning when it's freezing cold and dark, you will be trying to find wood, angry that someone burnt your stash.

2. Boil up water. Fill the giant kettle and then place it in the middle of the flames, being careful not to tip it over or burn yourself! When the water is bubbling, fill up as many flasks as you can. (A very useful metal bottle with a lid that keeps things hot.) Then, boil more water. You can never have too much boiled water.

3. Wake up your teammates (Charles, Richard, Rupert, and Keith). Have a hot drink together by the fire.

4. Most difficult job of all – GET THE REST OF THE CAMP MOVING!

The camel-handlers and the Chinese proudly wore large flashy watches, however, they all showed different times, and many didn't work at all. ODD!

China is such a huge country that it covers five different time zones. For unity, the time in the capital, Beijing, is used by the whole country. That was the time our watches were set to. It became obvious that the Chinese and the camel-handlers all had different ideas about what time it was!

Can you imagine how confusing that was?

It would be like your mum saying it's eight o'clock, your sister saying it's nine o'clock and you saying it's seven o'clock, so I am going back to bed!'

CONFUSING?

The camel-handlers ignored their watches completely, informing us, 'We get up when the sun comes up.' For them, this was the most natural way to lead their lives.

It made perfect sense; however it was not going to work on this expedition; we needed to get up before the sun and GET MOVING!

Every day we struggled to wake up the rest of the team.

It was a constant source of annoyance and frustration. Reluctantly, we had to accept the others were not really that bothered about crossing the desert!

Charles' research showed that the weather changed dramatically as autumn turned into winter. Temperatures plummet and more sandstorms occur.

I, for one, did not want to be in the desert when it was minus 30°C and a 'black out' because of a sandstorm. Even to me that didn't sound like fun! Our time in China was limited; return plane journeys were booked and people were expecting us back. Pushing the expedition on was the only way we could possibly succeed.

CHAPTER 21

Early Morning Call
Spicy Rice For Breakfast
Chasing Camels
Exploding Cookers

Try to imagine seeing our camp at about 05.30 in the morning; it's pitch black. Ok, you're going to need special goggles that help you see in the dark!

Dotted between the sand dunes, you can see little mounds of wriggling sleeping bags, like giant maggots, water containers and heaps of sacks and lots of camels just wandering around.

The fire starts to glow. You see headtorches bobbing around the desert as we call out, first quietly, and then, when no one moves, SHOUTING, 'Ni hao, Ni hao,' ('Hello! Hello!' in Mandarin), as we encouraged our fellow teammates to get moving.

Next, you see the fierce gas-burning cooker quite literally burst into action causing people to run for cover, fearing the possibility of an EXPLOSION!

Once the flame has settled down, the Chinese scientist, the happiest and most able chef, sets to work.

Lao Zhao, nicknamed 'Calculus', was the only person capable of calming the beast of a cooker, although even he was attacked by it once, needing treatment from me for a burn to his hand. He prepared a cooked breakfast from leftover rice and spices from the previous night's meal, throwing everything into a GIANT BLACK FRYING PAN.

On the open fire, a large kettle starts to boil the water for hot drinks and porridge. The porridge from the UK was already mixed with milk powder; just adding hot water makes a warming breakfast to start the day. Sitting on dusty sleeping mats, we squeezed up together to get close to the fire, stared into the flames and shovelled down porridge with lots of sugar. We needed the extra energy.

I always had the same breakfast – PORRIDGE!

For the first few days, the boys also had porridge, but before long they became more adventurous (hungry) and joined the Chinese eating spicy fried rice every morning!

With breakfast finished, the next thing you see is the camel-handlers attempting to round up the camels.

This was usually not very successful, however, they came up with a good trick. If they waved the giant blue tarpaulin (the one used for the Uyghur feast on the edge of the desert at the start), this got the camels' attention. The Uyghurs called out, frantically waved the tarpaulin, and then quickly emptied the split grain (camel food) in a line around the edge.

LOOK OUT!

Here they come, galloping in for their breakfast from all areas of the desert. An awesome sight, but NOT one to get mixed up in unless you are a camel! They pushed and shoved to get to their food. The camel-handlers tugged on their halters (the rope around their nose and head) to sit them down.

After a bit of squabbling – normal behaviour if you are a hungry camel, eventually thirty happy camels munched their breakfast.

NOW THE FUN REALLY BEGINS!

You are going to experience the organised chaos of loading thirty camels!

I hope you've had a big bowl of porridge.

You are going to need it.

First, catch your camel. Some are easier than others!

One by one, lead them in between various loads. Hopefully, the ropes are laid out ready.

The camel sits down, and the loads are lifted and tied into position. 📷

Sounds simple when I write it like that. Very occasionally, it was simple, but usually it involved shouting, screaming and sometimes laughing.

One person needs to attempt to control the camel by holding the halter round its head. We worked in pairs, two people on each side of a camel. Rupert could operate on his own, but for most of us the loads were too heavy.

I worked with Lao Zhao and learnt to count to three in Chinese 1 (yi); 2 (er); 3 (san): we lifted together on san. 📷

Camel sacks were the easiest; you threw them over the humps and secured them in place with rope.

The oblong water tins were heavy and awkward, with sharp pointy corners. The camels were not keen on carrying them.

The rope supplied by the camel-handlers was not ideal. Although thick, it was made from **cotton**.

DO NOT go climbing with this rope, it will break!

The camels quickly learnt that if they didn't want to budge, all they had to do was dig their heels in. They are strong and stubborn. We pulled on the ropes, the camels said NO and didn't move.

Can you guess what happened?

Yep... the rope broke!

Everyone fell over, and smiling camel 'legs it' to freedom! We then spend ten minutes chasing camels around and trying to fix the rope by tying giant knots!

Remember those stories about bad-tempered camels and spitting?

When you load camels in the morning, this is when you see them in action living up to their reputation. Keep your wits about you to avoid being hit by...

CAMEL BREAKFAST!

Even after weeks of practising, it still took at least two hours to load up. We tried hard to be ready for Charles' 09.30 departure; you can see now why we needed to get up so early. It was a constant battle to keep the expedition moving.

CHAPTER 22

Dashing Behind the Dunes

Gradually, we began to settle into a routine.

Charles studied his maps.

Rupert sorted out the communications.

Keith rushed around taking photos.

Richard maintained diplomatic relations, chatting to all team members, then reporting back to Charles. He carried around a BBC recording device as he gave a running commentary of what was going on, not forgetting to record our beloved noisy camels! The recording would be used to make a radio programme when and if we made it back to the UK!

I set up my 'drop in' clinic area.

The Uyghurs looked after the camels.

The Chinese prepared food.

Everyone was supposed to help with digging for water.

Our days were monotonous and predictable; the same thing day in day out, trudging along, one behind the other, up and down the sand dunes.

Some of the sand was so fine we waded through it above our knees!

It was almost as fine as talcum powder, or it was like very gritty wholegrain flour!

You must learn to live with the sand, welcome it in and say, 'Hello, sand, I don't mind you being everywhere in my eyes, ears, between my toes, in my mouth, and just about anywhere else you can imagine!'

Every drink and every mouthful of food had a certain crunch.

If you've been to a sandy beach or played in the sandpit at school when you were younger, you'll remember that it doesn't matter how careful you are, sand gets everywhere – and I mean EVERYWHERE!!!!

SAND, SAND, SAND and more SAND!

We were crossing a very big sandy desert. What did I expect? Get used to it; this sand is here to stay. After a few weeks, you just accepted it, even finding yourself chewing sand between your teeth as you walked along. I don't think this would be recommended by your dentist!

Obviously, sand gets in your boots, which is why you might see the rather funny sight of team members lying on their backs (another nickname... dead ants) waving their legs in the air and banging their feet together!

This is how to get sand out of your boots without taking them off for the hundredth time that day. BORING!

So, just to go over it again, in case I haven't said it enough, there's a lot of SAND.

Occasionally, we had some excitement, or at least a change from the dullness of just walking. One of the camels, usually Number 8, would refuse to move, break free, and gallop off, dumping his load somewhere in the desert.

This meant we had to stop. The camels rested and watched. I am certain they were laughing at us, as we ran around waving our arms and shouting. Camel Number 8 dashed about the desert avoiding capture: funny and a bit tragic. It always ended the same way: he gave up, exhausted. Sweating and angry we reloaded him. Number 8, nicknamed Einstein because of a tangle of mane that bounced in front of his rolling wild eyes, was only given water to carry once and never again.

Water was too precious for him to be trusted with. When not galloping around the desert, he was quiet and withdrawn.

It turned out that Einstein's disruptive behaviour was understandable; he had been separated from his mother before the age of three. Camels like to stay with their mums until they are three to five years old. Poor Einstein was too young to be in a camel train. Charles spoke to Barney in the support team, saying rather unkindly, 'We have a wild camel that must be replaced at the next resupply point. Please find a suitable replacement at one of the markets along the Silk Road.'

Back on the trail, I noticed that Charles, Richard, then Rupert, and finally Keith kept rushing off behind the dunes. Being boys, they were quite vocal about what was going on. They laughed and joked with each other as they shared stories of increasing diarrhoea and discomfort.

More nicknames were given to this episode, referred to as 'RUNNING FOR THE DUNES', DASHING TO THE DUNES' and 'THE SQUITS'!

You probably don't need me to explain what was going on!! Eventually, the boys plucked up courage and spoke to me. The most likely cause for the 'Squits' was a change in diet (travellers' diarrhoea). But, why wasn't I affected?

What were the boys doing that I wasn't?

Can you think what might have caused their problem?

I reminded everyone that losing fluid from your body increased the risk of dehydration.

The daytime temperature was well over 40°C.

VERY, VERY HOT. It was vital to keep hydrated.

'If liquid is coming out, guys, you have to put fluid back in.' I had tablets that slowed up diarrhoea, but if this was a bug it was best to get rid of it, ASAP.

It was a few days before we realised what caused the boys to keep 'DASHING TO THE DUNES' and the rather unpleasant 'SQUITS'!

Have you guessed?

CHAPTER 23

THE GIANT FRYING PAN

Why did the men have 'The Squits' and not me?

I am not complaining! But we needed to find the cause. I spoke to Charles about our daily routines to see if there were any clues. It had to be something they were eating.

You have probably worked it out already (I think the chapter title gave it away). The men always had porridge followed by fried rice. I never had the fried breakfast.

Rice was cooked in the GIANT FRYING PAN first in the evening and then again in the morning for breakfast! Charles decided he would keep an eye on the giant frying pan. In the evening, when Lao Zhao had tamed the exploding gas cooker, the giant pan was pulled from a dusty camel sack and cleaned using sand. This may sound a bit revolting, but sand is a really good way to clean plates and frying pans, although, probably don't use it on your parents' best non-stick pans!

After the evening meal, any rice not eaten was stored in a container for use at breakfast. The giant pan was put to one side. Sometime during the night, a camel-handler borrowed the pan and used it to cook food, and then... used it to water and feed the CAMELS!

Yes, that's right, the CAMELS!!!

Camels' mouths are not the most hygienic places!

Even if you really love camels, you would agree with this statement.

In the morning, the frying pan travelled back to the Chinese. Lao Zhao cooked the leftover rice, and then he fed the men!

'I've got it,' said Charles.

'It's that GIANT FRYING PAN. That's what's making us ill!'

A meeting was called to discuss camp hygiene.

Richard did his best to interpret.

Charles held up and waved around the frying pan, and said, 'This is to be used for humans.'

He then held up a shiny metal bucket and said, 'This is for camels.'

He demonstrated by putting it in front of one of the camels who looked at him as if to say, 'What are you silly people doing now?'

'Bucket for camels and frying pan for humans.

NO SHARING!'

Mystery solved!

CHAPTER 24

Dysentery in the Dunes

The boys dashing to the dunes reduced, so I assumed they were recovering. However, one person continued to suffer. Richard, nicknamed Little Bean; his tummy upset and running to the dunes continued.

'Little Bean' was usually seen trotting up and down beside the camel trains busily chatting to everyone and doing his best to keep us all working together.

This normally energetic 'full of beans' character was uncharacteristically quiet, withdrawn and getting slower and slower until one fateful day when he disappeared behind the last camel train, I assumed it was for another 'Dash to the Dunes.' Concerned for his wellbeing, I left my normal position with the first camel train and dropped back to keep an eye on him. A camel sack had slipped and needed repositioning. The last camel train stopped and I helped Mr Guo reload.

Far ahead, I could just make out Rupert and Charles, a mile or so in the distance, plotting the route to lead us through the sand mountains. The camel trains were scattered in dishevelled groups across the dunes. We started the day together, but it was never long before one group needed to stop because either a camel sack had slipped, was cutting in, or had been completely dumped.

And so it went on, all day, every day, stopping and starting.

Mr Guo and I dripping with sweat, struggled to reload the camel. Exhausted, and breathing heavily I gazed back through the shimmering heat haze.

Where was 'Little Bean'?

I couldn't see him; please, please appear from behind a dune!

There was not a sign of him.

I peered into the distance, desperately scanning the horizon.

Still nothing

'Mr Guo, you continue on with the camels, catch up with the others and tell Charles we have a problem. I will GO BACK to find Richard.'

GO BACK!!!!

I am not proud admitting this, I hesitated…

The last thing any of us wanted to do was to walk back over ground we had already covered.

When you cross a desert or walk to school, you do so one step at a time. I know it sounds obvious, but when you have hundreds of miles to go, you break it down into steps, each one being one step closer to finishing.

'The journey of a thousand miles starts with a single step.'

I was going to repeat some of those steps three times!!!

Get over it... Little Bean was in trouble; he needed help!

I started retracing our footsteps, stopping every now and then to look. Charles and Rupert were now out of sight, unaware of the situation. Eventually Mr Guo would catch up with the main team and let them know what had happened, but for now I was on my own in the middle of the desert trying to find 'Little Bean'.

Anxiously I felt for the water bottle on my belt and gave it a little shake. It's about half full let's hope that's enough for me to find him and get us back to safety. The heat from the sun beat down on my head, it felt like my brain was being fried. I started to think bad things, what if I don't find him, what if I do find him and he is too ill to move, what if there's a sandstorm, what if I get lost and run out of water. WHAT IF? ... HELP!

I had to give myself a good talking to... GET A GRIP, ELLIS (my surname) you can do this, you've got water and a compass, focus on what you need to do... this was a survival situation no time for tears or being pathetic.

FIND AND RESCUE RICHARD (Little Bean)!

Luckily, there was no wind blowing, so the track left by thirty camels was easy to follow. I looked carefully either side of the trail for any footprints that headed off behind a dune, but so far nothing. I walked further and further, glancing back over my shoulder at the disappearing camel train, until all I could see was sand dunes.

'That's it girl, you're on your own, in the DESERT OF DEATH and DESERT OF NO RETURN!'

HELP!

It's not a nice feeling being alone in a desert, I really had to believe that I would be able to find my way back. I remembered those Uyghur ladies right at the beginning of our adventure, who had cried and begged me not to go into the desert, I was beginning to wish I had listened to them!

After what seemed like hours of walking BACK, I started thinking another WHAT IF... what if I've missed him!

I can't have missed him... can I?

I was beginning to seriously doubt myself and was thinking of turning back, when in the distance I spotted something.

A tiny little heap under a tamarisk bush.

Was that him?

Was that 'Little Bean?'

It didn't look good. I broke into a sort of run/walk. I needed to get to him fast. He was curled up lying on his side and looked terrible. I checked his pulse: WEAK and RAPID. Whatever else was going on, he was dehydrated.

He did a good job at pretending to be OK, politely chatting, however, he was talking rubbish. Well, not rubbish. He was talking about his honeymoon and his wife, Anthea. The worrying thing was, he thought I was her!

We sat together in the tiny bit of shade cast by the twiggy tamarisk bush. I got various things out of my rucksack and set to work. I made up a drink with special sugars and salts (you might have had this sort of medicine if you were poorly with diarrhoea when you were little).

I had to insist he drank it.

He wasn't keen, but the option of me putting up an intravenous infusion (needle in his arm with a tube which fluid goes through) he liked even less

Next, I consulted my trusty medical book. I flicked through the pages looking for **amoebic dysentery**!!!

In this sort of situation, you can't say, 'Oh, let's see how it goes.'

NO, that would be a bad move.

You also can't say, 'Let's send some tests off to the desert lab!'

NO, that will not work either.

Look at all the signs and symptoms and treat your patient (Little Bean) as if it's the worst thing it could possibly be.

My book and I agreed; AMOEBIC DYSENTERY!

I rummaged around in my waistcoat pockets and found some very strong antibiotics. I explained my plan. With a lot of encouragement, he swallowed the very large tablets. The sooner he started, the sooner they would get to work.

I had to be quite bossy. 'KEEP DRINKING.'

After some time, his pulse returned to a normal level, and he started to make a bit more sense.

The daylight was fading and, although I had my headtorch, I definitely did not want to be stumbling around the desert in the dark.

That would not be fun!

My patient dragged himself to his feet, and for the first time I noticed how small and vulnerable he looked. We found the trail left by the camels and started our meandering journey back towards the teams.

Somehow 'Little Bean' managed to make a joke about the fact we were following camel poo to lead us back to our friends! (That's actually quite funny now, but I am not sure if I laughed then!) Our progress was slow, as we stopped and started. When we rested I insisted he drank his medicine. All the time I was hoping Charles or Rupert would appear over the next Dune and give us a cheery wave, but I guess they were busy and didn't realise how bad the situation was. The sun was going down quickly, darkness would soon be here, please, please let me see the light of a campfire soon. I have never been happier to see SMOKE! Richard and I hugged, happy and enormously relieved to see the chaos of camels, water containers, bags and people dashing around digging waterholes and preparing supper. We staggered quietly into camp, with 'Little Bean' pretending everything was fine.

He was fooling no one.

I explained to Charles how I found Richard, collapsed and delirious, under a bush. And that I thought he had amoebic dysentery.

I showed Charles my treasured green and yellow book.

This is the most important book I have. It's

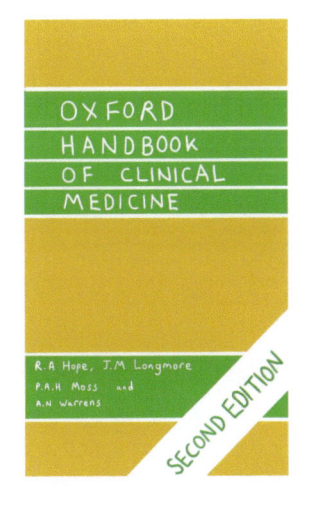

the **Oxford Handbook of Clinical Medicine**, and it goes everywhere with me. I had to make Charles understand 'Little Bean' was seriously ill. 'We must get him out of the desert. He needs hospital treatment if he is to have a chance of surviving this.'

The first resupply was still a few days away. Rescuing Richard before then was impossible. There was no way the support team could get to us as we were still deep in the sand mountains and needed to find our way out.

The dangers we faced had suddenly become very real.

It was up to us to look after Richard and get him to the resupply, from where he could be rescued.

Rupert made a hollow in the sand and lined it with a soft mat followed by a sleeping bag, saying, 'It looks like I've just dug you a shallow grave.'

Despite being very poorly 'Little Bean' managed a smile at Rupert's attempt at a joke. By digging down into the sand it created a soft area just below the surface that gave some protection from the wind that blew most nights. (sandstorm)

We wrapped Richard up in his sleeping bag and helped him drink and take more enormous tablets.

The next day he was no worse but not a lot better. Pale, weak and struggling to put one foot in front of the other, he reluctantly accepted he needed to ride one of the stronger more trustworthy camels.

CHAPTER 25

Red Mountains in Sight

We tumbled down the last of the sand mountains and, to our relief, found a flat area. The ground had a crusty, dry covering. Walking was easier, and we made good progress.

For as far as you could see, the desert surface was littered with rocks of various shapes and sizes. For weeks, all we had seen was SAND, SAND and more SAND.

It was exciting to see something different.

As you already know, I am a bit odd. Here's another strange thing. I love collecting interesting stones or pebbles from the beach. Excitedly, I picked up small stones that caught my eye: interesting shapes, colours and some that even sparkled! We compared our finds, marvelled at them, and then slipped them safely into our pockets. 📷 In the distance, the long red ridge of the Mazartagh Mountains – an extinct volcano, loomed up for all to see. 📷

Ancient stories and legends spoke of treasure that possibly lay here… gold and diamonds!!

Perhaps my pockets were full of DIAMONDS!

I still have those stones; maybe I should get them checked out!

The camel-handlers also knew the stories.

That night, as we camped in the foothills of the red mountain, they abandoned digging for water and went in search of treasure. Searching for diamonds was far more exciting than digging waterholes!

The following morning, when Charles discovered the camels had not been given water, he was angry, and the camels were thirsty!

He called a team meeting and told us all off, saying, 'You have neglected your duties and let the camels down! Putting it simply, IF THE CAMELS DIE, WE WILL DIE. Only Richard is allowed to ride a camel today.'

Several team members had ridden camels during the last fourteen days, saying, 'Their legs and feet are too sore to walk.' At the start of the journey, each camel carried a heavy load: either water, camel food, rations or equipment.

As each day went by, the amount that needed carrying went down; camels and humans were eating the food and drinking the water.

Sometimes, a lucky camel would find itself without a load.

However, it wasn't long before some of the less motivated team members (that's another way to say 'LAZY'!) spotted an opportunity to rest their legs and jumped on the back of a camel!

So, when Charles said, 'No one will ride today,' the camels were happy, and those people who liked to ride (NOT ME) were annoyed and grumpy.

The national flags of China and the United Kingdom flapped in the wind as we headed towards the first resupply. Unusually, the Chinese team came to the front. Perhaps they sensed a film crew in the distance. This annoyed Charles and the rest of us. 'Little Bean', who thankfully was responding to the antibiotics, advised Charles to let the Chinese team lead and have their moment of glory. This was, after all, their country and, without their happiness and support, the expedition could quite easily be stopped.

The camels had a spring in their step; many with no sacks or people to carry. They walked faster, almost trotting; perhaps they could smell the fresh food and water ahead.

In the distance, we spotted an odd cloud on the horizon in the otherwise clear blue sky. It was moving closer and closer.

Was it a dust storm or…?

Two bright lights beamed out and then we heard the sound of an engine! From his vantage point on top of the camel, Richard shouted excitedly, 'The cavalry has arrived!' Charles and Rupert's handheld radio transmitters crackled into life. 'Music, I can hear music,' said Charles. 'Military marching music.'

Out of the dusty cloud appeared the vehicles, 'Bella' closely followed by 'Thomas.' We had not expected to see the support team yet. 'Bella' was driven by Barney with lights flashing and Union Jack **pennant** (small triangular flag) flying high from the radio antenna.

I was almost tearful seeing the flag and then hearing the music. Don't worry, I soon pulled myself together when I remembered that the support team had CHOCOLATE!

Barney told us how they decided to drive into the desert and surprise us. The official resupply point was still another fifteen miles away. The Chinese team were disappointed. Their trucks were unable to make it through the soft sand. We gathered excitedly around the vehicles. It felt like years since we had seen each other, but was in fact just fourteen days! We hugged and laughed, happy and relieved to see our friends.

Mark and Anne produced tea, coffee and various treats, including CHOCOLATE from the back of their vehicles as they shared their supplies with everyone.

Barney was expecting to take Richard out of the desert, however 'Little Bean' had other ideas. The antibiotics were working, he was feeling a little better, and he wanted to finish the first phase of the expedition with the crossing team. Keith also turned down the chance of a lift. Eager to get on, Charles called festivities to a close. With a tooting of horns and arms waved out of windows, the two vehicles left and headed back to the camp at Mazartagh.

The sound of military music faded into the distance.

Charles had warned us that he planned an extra-long day of walking: twice the distance normally covered.

So instead of about fifteen miles, we walked more like thirty! By doing this it meant we reached the resupply area one day early, thereby giving us two days' REST!

Stumbling through the darkness, it felt like the end was never coming; the sun had set hours ago. In the distance were some faint lights – the Mazartagh camp.

Exhausted and thirsty, we were greeted by both support teams; vehicle lights beamed and flashed into the desert, blinding us as we walked towards them. Mr Guo's team were now much happier and sprang into life. The television crews started filming... the first people in living history to walk this two-hundred-mile stretch of the Taklamakan Desert.

A worrying and rather depressing thought popped into my head – only another eight hundred miles to go!

DON'T THINK ABOUT THAT!

Let's find the support team's CHOCOLATE.

CHAPTER 26

Who's Been Crying? Rupert Gets a Hair Cut

We camped at the foot of the mountain ridge behind some dunes, most importantly, next to an unexpected but very welcome large pool of water.

The **Hotan River** carries water from the **Kunlun Mountains** in the south. The river flows usually once a year for just a few days in the summer. Melted snow from the mountains flows down and out into the desert and then vanishes deep into the sand. We were lucky that the pool of water had remained. Although it was rapidly disappearing, now thirty thirsty camels had arrived.

The camels were happy and not budging.

Standing beside them, you could hear water sloshing into their empty stomachs.

Next morning we had a lie-in, like you do perhaps on a Sunday? But not for long as we had lots to do and an **ancient fort** that needed exploring.

Let me explain about Mazartagh in case you have imagined a busy town with shops (that would have been nice!) Years ago it was a busy village but now was abandoned. There were derelict huts, a few wild goats and a dusty, sandy (obviously) track that linked the area to the Southern Silk Road, over a hundred miles away. This was the route our support teams had driven up.

Our Chinese friends were interviewed by the (**CCTV**) Chinese Central Television, recounting stories of heroic deeds and how they had battled through the sand mountains. Lao Zhao, the scientist, spoke about the British team, our determination, and that only two people had walked the whole way (SO FAR!); both were British, and wait for it... big shock,

'One of them,' he said, 'is "a WOMAN"!'

Now, who could that be?

When the TV company heard this news, they stopped filming the Chinese men and instead wanted to talk to the 'British woman.'

When they interviewed me, they kept asking, 'Is it true you have been CRYING a lot?'

What an odd question. 'NO!'

I mean, it's ok to cry, but I really hadn't been crying, so why would they ask that?

All I could think was that in their embarrassment the men might have said, 'Oh, yes. She's walked, but she does cry all the time.' As you can imagine, that made me even more determined to continue walking. How annoying would it be if one day I heard in the news that someone had become the first woman to walk a thousand miles across the Taklamakan.

NO!

This was my chance, and I was determined to keep walking. I was doing it for QUEEN and COUNTRY! Well, not really – ok, perhaps a bit. Mainly, I was doing it for ME and more importantly for YOU!

Anyway, let's not get overconfident; there's still a very, very long way to go! Remember – one step at a time!

The camel-handlers, who were quite shy, avoided the cameras. Instead, they sat around talking, eating, and preparing for the next part of the journey.

They also decided to cut their hair.

Emir one of the older Uyghurs produced a very sharp, dangerous-looking **cut-throat razor** and proceeded to shave all the Uyghurs' heads.

They roared with laughter when Rupert asked Emir to shave his head as well! Within minutes, Rupert's curly hair lay on the desert floor.

📷 Funny photo.

I reminded them to wear their hats. 'We don't want sunburnt heads now that you are all BALD!'

'Rupert is turning into an Uyghur,' said Mark.

This statement caused much laughter. Despite our language barriers, we were beginning to form a strong friendship. We liked the Uyghur camel-handlers and strangely they seemed to like us.

CHAPTER 27

Exploring an Ancient Fort

Perched up high on the old volcanic ridge and built of red sandstone, were the remains of an ancient fort. 📷 It was built in the 6th century (1500 years ago!!) by Tibetan soldiers – an outpost that marked a trading route through the desert. Charles had studied history and archaeology at university and couldn't wait to explore the ruin. Richard, although still poorly, was determined not to miss out on this adventure and made one last big effort to climb the slopes. 📷

We carried the BBC Radio device and a video camera loaned by a southwest TV company, talking and filming as we went. Scrambling up the slopes to explore the fort, I thought of the explorer Sir **Aurel Stein** who visited a hundred years ago.

We looked around, careful not to disturb the archaeological site, but you couldn't help seeing things that were scattered on the surface. Mark found a wooden comb and I picked up a flat wooden stick with very unusual writing on it.

To think that these things were thousands of years old. We carefully wrapped up the artefacts for safe keeping.

SOME HISTORY FOR YOU:
Aurel Stein, in his 1907 expedition, excavated a large rubbish heap at the site. Believe it or not, you can find out a lot about people by looking at their rubbish! He discovered over a thousand military documents written on wood. These are now in the British Library. He also found smaller things: a comb, a shoe, arrows, dice and a pen. You can see them in the British Museum and the Victoria and Albert Museum. Some pieces are of Buddhist origins and date from two to three thousand years ago. Research into these ancient documents continues to this day.

Back at camp, I helped Richard pack. The Chinese military support vehicle would take him to the nearest hospital on the Silk Road. Richard was a crucial part of our team. His calm and thoughtful manner and the way he made everyone feel important would be missed.

Esa Polta, the lead camel-handler, who was about the age of your grandad, was also causing concern. He had fallen a few days ago, landing heavily on his left side. It's a long way down from the back of a camel to the desert floor.

Quite a BUMP!

I gently examined him, but he definitely needed further medical help and some x-rays.

I spoke with Charles explaining that I didn't think Esa Polta's leg was broken, but that he seemed to have lost the will to go on. I had the distinct feeling he didn't want to continue his desert adventure.

Charles spoke patiently and kindly to Esa Polta. He was a proud and thoughtful man and told Charles that travelling into the Taklamakan Desert and sitting on the highest sand mountain 📷 had been a dream come true, but now he was tired, in pain, and wished to go home to his family.

He said, 'to DIE!'

This last statement, as you can imagine, upset everyone. Esa believed his journey had been to see the desert of his forefathers (ancient people) one last time before he died!!

Rosa, one of the younger camel-handlers, was Esa's nephew. He stood anxiously beside his uncle. The decision was easy: Esa must leave; he needed to be checked out at the hospital and Rosa would go with him. We were upset saying goodbye to them. Over the last few weeks Esa Polta had entertained us with stories of lost civilisations and treasures buried in the sand. Rosa was tearful; he didn't want to miss out on the adventure and, probably more importantly, any GOLD or diamonds that might be found.

Esa and Rosa joined Richard in the Chinese support truck. We waved them off.

In just over two weeks people from very different cultures had become close friends. Not surprisingly, a few tears were shed, and not just by me!

Even Rupert had to walk away pretending he had sand in his eyes. Not that old trick; 'I've got something in my eye'!

With a roar of engines and in a cloud of dust, the truck turned south and headed out of the desert towards the Silk Road. We stood silently staring until eventually, far in the distance perched on the horizon, the truck was just a small dot.

Rosa, Esa and 'Little Bean' had started a new adventure and one that hopefully would lead them back to the safety of their families.

We, on the other hand, still had a desert to cross!

CHAPTER 28

Roast and Ski Sunday

With no Esa Polta, we needed someone to be in charge of the camels. Kirim reluctantly took up the position. At the next resupply two more Uyghurs would join our team. One, an experienced camel farmer, would bring ten fresh camels to replace any that were showing signs of exhaustion or just too grumpy to go on.

WORK TO BE DONE:

Empty out the camel sacks and calculate how much food and water were needed for the next part of the journey.

Our two support vehicles parked up next to each other, forming the heart of the British camp.

The support team decided we needed looking after and busied themselves bringing us cups of hot sweet tea. Barney had everything under control.

Francis looked relaxed, was smiling more and, of course, was not wearing a suit!

Anne surprised everyone by miraculously producing a ROAST!

Roast lamb! (more likely a scrawny old goat), roast potatoes, and cabbage! In the shadow of a red mountain, an ancient fort, sand dunes and roaming camels, we sat down at a table with chairs to eat a roast that even included CABBAGE!!!! It seems there is no escaping cabbage, even in a desert in China!

To top it all, Barney opened a bottle of something that fizzed and popped...

'Amazing.' We all cheered! 'Champagne and Sunday roast.' Charles stood up, raised a glass, and said, 'To us all. We have crossed two hundred miles of the infamous Taklamakan Desert. Here's to the next eight hundred miles.' We all laughed. You have probably realised by now that we have a strange sense of humour. I mean, is it funny to think you have eight hundred miles to go? Not really!

This is my excuse; people who have dangerous and difficult jobs like soldiers, doctors, nurses, police officers and explorers often develop an odd sense of humour to help them deal with bad stuff.

I doubt the thought of walking eight hundred miles is making you laugh. Actually, it's not making me laugh at the moment but here's something that might.

The Chinese and Uyghurs already thought we were a bit odd! It was, after all, our idea to cross the desert – the desert that had been quite happy sitting in China minding its own business with no one wanting to cross it for hundreds of years!

Until Charles had a light bulb moment!

'I've got it! Let's cross the Taklamakan Desert!'

Rupert, Mark and I just followed him, which probably means we are also bonkers!!

Just in case anyone had any doubts about how silly we really were we decided to do something strange: well, strange for a sandy desert.

Poking out of camel sacks since the beginning at Markit were several long thin flat planks. Bet you can't guess what they were?

SKIS!

Rupert and Mark went SKIING in the desert!!!

Yes, skiing!!

A World First never seen before, and unlikely to be seen again. They attached the skis to their boots, and to much laughter, entertained everyone as they attempted to ski down sand dunes.

Apparently, there are deserts in the world where cross-country skis work better than walking.

The Taklamakan was not one of them! Rupert said it was 'The wrong sort of sand,' which made us all laugh.

The Uyghurs looked on in amusement and disbelief; they'd never seen anything like it!

The Chinese team shook their heads.

ECCENTRIC, SILLY, BONKERS, even BRAVE?

You choose.

During the night, one of the camels decided that walking another eight hundred miles was not for him; he legged it to freedom, escaping to who knows where or what. Charles was angry but smiled when he thought about what could happen. The escaped camel might walk into an Uyghur's yard, which would be like you waking up and finding a Rolls Royce in your garden. For an Uyghur family somewhere on the edge of the desert, their luck and lives would change for ever. Camels are worth a lot of money especially fit, brave camels.

Keith, the photographer, stayed with the support team to record their journey and give his feet time to heal.

Mark (Kipper) joined the crossing team as interpreter, support navigator and radio operator.

The camels too were saying goodbye to Einstein (Number 8). Hopefully, they were encouraging him to behave a little better; no one wants to buy a misbehaving camel! With luck, he'd end up on a farm with older female camels who'd look after him. We said goodbye and good luck to Number 8. He was replaced by a camel from the local area.

After two days' rest, it was time to get going.

Walking boots back on, we loaded up, waved to our pals and set off back into the sand dunes.

We travelled along dry river beds lined with tall poplar trees. The brown and orange leaves reminded us it was now autumn and we needed to get a move on.

CHAPTER 29

Camel Wounds and I Get a Nickname!

Rupert first noticed the problem. A drip of something on the desert floor, that was not water. The liquid ran down the leg of one of the camels. He stopped the camel train to investigate and pulled up the edge of a saddle. What he found was not nice.

'That's revolting. It looks like some of the camels have sores under their saddles.'

Mark and I checked our camels and discovered more wounds.

How could we have let this happen?

It's basic stuff. You would never leave a saddle on a pony overnight. So why had we been doing that to our camels?

We had followed the camel-handlers' instructions, believing they knew best.

Charles was furious.

'We can't stop now, we must push on, and we will make a full assessment later.'

That night, as we dragged ourselves into camp, Charles instructed, 'Remove all saddles. Rupert and Carolyn will make a full inspection.'

I am ashamed to say that for the first time in weeks the saddles were removed revealing a grim sight. Terrible wounds had been caused by heavy loads and inadequate padding in the saddles. Some poor camels had deep cuts into their humps where ropes had quite literally sliced into them. The wounds were infected and crawling with maggots.

Ten camels needed attention, but who was going to help them?

You know this bit of the story; it's ME. I patched up our camels and got the nickname, 'CAMEL DOC.'

Working with camels at a zoo in Devon was not the best preparation for dealing with maggot-infested wounds, but it was better than nothing.

I remembered the advice from a friend at my hockey club – an experienced equine (horse) vet. She suggested, 'Treat a camel the same as a horse, and as for wounds, it doesn't matter if they are on huge hairy camels or soldiers in hospital. Treatment remains the same.'

CLEAN the wounds and cut away bad stuff! Rupert spoke calmly, stroking the camels as he reassured them we wanted to help.

Quietly, I explained everything I was doing. Camels are bright creatures; they seemed to understand that we meant no harm.

The men watched me work, occasionally remarking how revolting it was or making silly jokes.

I remained focused and determined to help our camels; without them we were in trouble.

And besides, I had grown fond of some of them. (Not the spitting ones!)

I think the men were surprised, even shocked for the following reasons:

1. So far, I had walked all the way.

2. Not only did I fix the men, but now I fixed the camels, dealing with maggots and pus!

Perhaps they were finally thinking, 'Ok, she is a woman, but actually she's quite tough and deserves her place on the team.'

Go to website thecameldoc.com for a real life photo

CHAPTER 30

'Hello Taklamakan'

Other camp routines continued.

Mark spoke on the radio to the support team, updating them on our journey, our health, and gruesome details of camel wounds! 📷

The support team had their own problems. Stuck for two days in a sandy bog (sinking sand) in a not-so-dry river bed! 📷

Fortunately, soldiers from a nearby army camp came to their rescue and pulled them out with a giant bulldozer. 📷

Rupert set up the **global satellite dish** and waited patiently to see if anyone contacted us. He used the time to show me how to operate the **satellite mobile phone**. Each of the four members of the British crossing team had a lead role on the expedition:

Navigator;
Communication (radio);
Translator;
Medic.

But it was also important we could do each other's jobs just in case one of us was injured, unwell, lost or worse!

We laughed at the word 'mobile phone', as Rupert dragged it across the sand. The satellite phone, one of the very first of its kind, was on loan from a company keen for it to be tested in the harsh environment of the desert.

All equipment had to endure extreme variations in temperature, lots of SAND, and the occasional dump onto the desert floor as a camel threw another sack off: a challenging test for any piece of high-tech machinery.

Keith started the trip with eight amazing cameras. Several were now broken. The more technical the gadget, the sooner it broke. My camera was old; it had a roll of film inside. Perhaps ask your grandparents to explain about these cameras. It still worked, but made a rather worrying scratchy, grating sound, and guess what was causing that? Yep, you're right. It was SAND!

Not ideal. My photos all had scratches across them!

Thanks to new technology, those marks made by the sand have been removed although, if you look closely, you might still see little scratches on some photos.

The so-called mobile phone was a large heavy box with a phone attached. Rupert could just about carry it.

It had an aerial that looked like a big black umbrella.

The phone was powered by a noisy generator that spluttered away, producing a nasty black smoke that curled off over the dunes. We were happy when we switched it off and peace returned to the desert.

Rupert pointed into the night sky at what looked like a shooting star, but was, in fact, a solitary satellite – our link with the outside world. Back in the UK, certain people had our special telephone number and knew the times we listened for a call.

Into the desert night came a strange ringing sound.

Camels and humans pricked up their ears and waited expectantly. Rupert grabbed the phone and said,

Everyone fell about laughing.

It was Bella from London, who wanted the latest news from the expedition. It was her job then to update Buckingham Palace, our families and the national papers.

'Please let me speak to Bella.' I was desperate. I just needed to hear a female voice, a friend, someone to reassure me I wasn't losing the plot.

Bella chatted and made me smile. We joked about the men and the antics of the crossing.

The next call was for Charles. He spoke with the **BBC World Service** recording a radio interview to be broadcast later in the week.

The third call was a regular weekly contact from a national newspaper. First, they spoke to

Charles, asking how the expedition was going; then they wanted to speak to me! This usually annoyed me because they always asked the same questions.

1. Have you fallen out with the boys?

2. Worse than that, they asked, have you fallen in LOVE with any of them?
 NO!

We have a desert to cross! Did they think we were in a Jane Austen novel and Charles or Rupert was Mr Darcy!!!

NO!

Don't get me wrong, the boys were ok (most of the time)... sometimes they told silly jokes, which got rather annoying! 📷

We were more like a big family: one sister with lots of brothers who were sometimes a bit irritating!

The reporters wanted something more interesting than SAND, SAND, SAND and us being thirsty all of the time. They wanted drama and excitement to sell their papers.

During the first phase of the expedition, a Sunday Newspaper published a story and the headline was,

'BRITISH EXPLORERS STRUGGLE TO SURVIVE IN DESERT OF DEATH.'

Journalists knocked on my mother's door, saying, 'Your daughter's dying of thirst in the desert. How do you feel about that?!!!'

Unfazed by their questions, she said, 'I am sure they will be fine. Over the years I have accepted that she just likes doing dangerous things.'

Thanks Mum.

CHAPTER 31

New Recruits: 10 x Camels; 2 x Uyghurs; 1 x Archaeologist; 1 x Artist.

The camel train snaked through the dunes towards the next resupply at Tongguzbasti. One of the camel-handlers, Emir, called out in excitement. He had spotted two Uyghur men riding mules, looking after a herd of goats. They wore thick coats and tall black fur hats and their faces were tanned and wrinkled from years of exposure to the desert. 📷 You might be thinking that's a bit strange, why are they wearing thick coats and fur hats in a hot desert? Forgive me if you already know this, but I need to explain because a grownup who read this didn't realise that hot deserts are very cold at night. Here is the reason why: sand grains are strange they are slippery and dry and not able to absorb heat. During the day they heat up and radiate the heat back into the air making it very hot. When the sun goes down the heat rises up, up and away because there are no clouds to act like a blanket and keep the heat down… so at night it is often freezing cold.

The goat herdsman smiled and their goats peered at us, bleated then bounced and skipped away, hiding behind tamarisk bushes unsure whether to be excited or scared. Seeing twenty-nine large raggedy camels (remember, one camel legged it at the last resupply) and a rather dishevelled group of strange-looking humans was enough to send anyone running to hide.

The goat herders exchanged formal greetings with our camel-handlers and then shook hands with everyone, smiling and bowing. Amazed at our journey, they praised the camel-handlers, saying they were brave heroes.

They led us towards the village of Tongguzbasti, passing traditional desert houses built of wood, branches and reeds. 📷 Our guides were intrigued to hear that a British woman, a medic, was part of the team. They bowed, shook my hand and gave me a toothy smile, or should I say toothless smile. I don't think there are many dentists in the desert.

As we walked into the tiny village, colourfully dressed children ran along beside us, shouting and cheering. 📷 Our arrival caused quite a commotion; villagers gathered around, patting and stroking our camels and stared inquisitively at us. We were possibly the first **Westerners** that many of them had seen. Smiling and shaking hands, we were honoured to receive so much attention. I guess it's not every day twenty-nine camels and a bunch of British, Chinese and Uyghur explorers stagger into your village.

Welcomed by the village elders, we were shown to an area to sit. It seemed they had been expecting us.

Women dressed in vibrantly coloured traditional costume danced whilst men played music on ancient instruments.

These kind desert people had very little, but what they did have they wished to share with us, providing us with a feast of locally produced food and drink.

How did they know so much about us, even knowing some of our names?! Although in translation the names had changed slightly Charles was Chas, Rupert was Rumper, I became Karola! We laughed but felt honoured that our names, even if they were slightly wrong, were known by so many. Curious to find out how the people knew about the expedition, Charles asked Zhang, the Chinese interpreter, who spoke Uyghur to ask the village elders.

They told him, 'We have one television in our village hut. It was given to us by the Chinese government so that important news and information from Beijing (2000 miles away) can be heard even in the most remote villages of the desert.' And they said, 'Your expedition is headline news.'

Apparently, we were famous throughout China, which was quite a cool thought. Charles didn't want us getting big-headed so reminded us, 'There's still a long way to go: seven hundred miles to be precise!'

Thanks for that, Charles.

You really know how to cheer a girl up!

We were joined by ten new camels supplied by a farm on the Silk Road. The new recruits were led into the desert by two Uyghurs: Suleiman, a camel farmer, and another, Abdul Rene. They joined the crossing team.

Charles announced, 'The wounded and weaker camels will be exchanged. They have been amazing, but it is time for them to be rested and go back to their families.'

We said good bye and good luck to nine of our camels and said hello to the new ones.

We also welcomed Krishna, a young Cambridge graduate who wanted to study the ancient sites of the desert. He travelled with the support team.

Paul, the expedition artist, joined the crossing team to record desert life in sketches and watercolours.

Once again, we calculated rations and water for the next phase. I was annoyed to discover that cold weather gear and some food from the UK suppliers had been left behind by the support truck. In these situations, Rupert was always calmer than me, saying, 'It's a hundred and fifty miles away; nothing can be done about it now. Let's just recalculate our food supplies and eat more rice... we have plenty of rice.'

Everyone groaned at the thought of MORE RICE!

The camels had split grain everyday so it only seemed fair we should eat rice every day! Then I remembered we had loads of POT NOODLES! Perfect when it's cold and you can't be bothered to cook. Just boil up water, add to the pot and hey presto: hot spicy NOODLES – delicious!

The news had spread that the expedition had a team medic, and it wasn't long before I was facing a long line of Uyghur mothers holding babies. They waited patiently hoping to be seen by the 'Camel Doc'! 📷

It's important that I remind you that we only had limited medical supplies. Anxiously, I began my unexpected baby clinic. What a relief to find that the little bundles of smiling babies were healthy; a little vitamin deficiency due to diet but other than that were fit and well.

I loved meeting the bouncing babies and their adoring mothers. Carefully, I examined every child, listening to their chests and praising them to their proud mums.

The mothers left, clutching their colourful bundles, happy that the British woman had held their babies and congratulated them on having healthy, adorable children.

CHAPTER 32

Ropes, Knives and 'BP' Needs Stitches!

At night, the camel-handlers cut rope, making halters for the camels. They talked and laughed together as they sliced the thick cotton rope with their sharp long KNIVES.

They pulled the blades towards them as they cut!!!

NOT a good idea! DO NOT TRY THIS AT HOME!

One night, the inevitable happened. Abdul (BP) pulled the blade upwards. The knife slipped and cut into his face. A shout went up from the Uyghur camp and the 'Camel Doc' was called into action.

His friends peered out from the darkness, oohing as I cleaned, stitched and patched up BP's face. Narrowly missing his eye, he had made an impressive deep slice into his cheek.

Why did these things always happen at night?

In the cold desert night, with my headtorch shining brightly, I repaired the wound. It made a nice change to be looking after a human and not a camel. At least BP didn't kick or spray his breakfast over me.

He was a regular attender at my clinics.

Whenever I patched up a wound or pulled out a rotten tooth, he gazed into my eyes and said, 'Ella yukshee' ('Very beautiful' in Uyghur.)

Rupert, Mark and Charles teased me, saying, 'We think BP is falling in love. You will have a romance to tell the reporters about.'

The men laughed, but I knew BP's loving looks meant something else.

He did gaze into my eyes and say, 'Ella yukshee' (Very beautiful) 📷, however, what the boys didn't see was that BP tapped my boots. He was saying my boots were very beautiful and probably about the right size for him.

179

So it was not the 'Camel Doc' he was falling in love with, it was my walking boots!

Well, he couldn't have them... yet.

We still had a desert to cross!

The Uyghurs happily came to my desert clinics with coughs, colds, wounds, toothache and anything that was bothering them, but the Chinese preferred to use their own **traditional medicine**. They were suspicious of both Western medicine and me!

I respected their beliefs but was always happy to help them. I shared my knowledge, medicine and carefully explained treatments. With time, they learnt to trust me.

We said goodbye to the goat herdsmen, their families and the colourfully- dressed children of Tongguzbasti and headed once more back into the dunes.

One hundred and forty miles until the next resupply!

CHAPTER 33

Sea Water or Swimming Pool Water?

Back in the desert, Suleiman quickly demonstrated his knowledge and skill. He highlighted what we already suspected – that the so-called camel-handlers from Markit had very little, and in most cases, no idea how to look after camels! The downside was that getting ready in the mornings now took even longer. Suleiman wanted to oversee all loading to prevent further injuries.

It turned out that Kirim was a lorry driver, BP a mechanic and the others had no experience of working with animals.

We were disappointed that we had been deceived, although we didn't blame the Uyghurs for wanting to come on the adventure. They were brave to have volunteered, encouraged no doubt by Esa Polta's stories of lost treasures and GOLD. Suleiman's knowledge was welcomed and he was immediately promoted to chief camel-handler. This pleased Kirim and the others who had been trying their best but were struggling.

At last someone looking after the camels actually knew what they were doing!

Each morning, before loading the silver containers, Rupert carefully dispensed water.

Every member of the crossing party was given two litres for drinking.

The water was poured into various bottles attached to our belts. To make certain the water was safe to drink, we added two purification tablets to each bottle, shook it up, and waited thirty minutes. We now had safe drinking water… however there was a catch! By mistake, have you ever swallowed swimming pool water? We all have. That's what our water tasted like!

Every time I sipped from the bottle on my belt, I was reminded of warm swimming pool water. Never again will I take for granted turning on a tap and having fresh, clean drinking water pour out. Even when we added various flavoured powders to disguise the taste, it still tasted of chlorine. No point in complaining.

The choice was swimming pool water or risk an upset stomach and more dashing behind the dunes!

On his first night in the desert, Paul, the artist, said with concern, 'Oh, that's not nice, my food has sand in it.'

We all looked at him and then fell about laughing.

Paul had just discovered what we had known for many weeks. All food and drink had an unmistakable sandy crunch to it.

Camels are designed to tolerate sand with nostrils that can close, bushy eyebrows and two rows of very thick eye lashes. Humans are not. We had to learn to live with it, not fight against it, and also accept being thirsty most of the time!

Two days from the last resupply, Rupert started pouring the fresh water into our bottles. Mark took a swig and spat it out – an odd reaction. I had a drink and quickly did the same. This was not swimming pool water. Much worse – it was SALTY WATER!

Ok, so you've tasted swimming pool water, now have you ever, again by mistake, had a mouthful of sea water?

HORRID.

Well, that's what the new water tasted like and we were supposed to drink it!!!

Mark spoke with Charles. 'We have a problem with the water collected from the so called **'sweet well'** at Tongguzbasti… it's SALTY.'

'Test all the containers.'

Mark and I tasted the water and marked the good and bad containers. After more calculating, we nervously agreed there was probably just about enough good water.

The salty water would need to be used for cooking and, in an absolute emergency, we might have to drink it!

Charles sat on the desert floor with his head in his hands. 'Another lesson learnt the hard way. I assumed because the villagers drank the water, it must be ok.' It turns out that just like our camels can tolerate salty water, the Uyghur desert people, through necessity, have developed the ability to drink brackish (salty) water. So, when the village people offered to share their water, they did so believing it was good for all to drink. However, the British and Chinese teams struggled to drink the salty water. Even when flavoured with lots of orange juice powder, it still tasted disgusting!

WHAT have we learnt?

1. Don't assume because someone says they are a camel-handler, that they are.

2. Don't assume because other people say the water is good, that it is.

3. DON'T ASSUME ANYTHING!!!!
   ALWAYS, ALWAYS CHECK IT YOURSELF.

CHAPTER 34

Very Thirsty Camels

We had gone three days without finding water.

Reaching the top of one huge sand mountain, we looked into the valley hoping to see something different. 📷 A ripple of excitement passed back down through the camel train. Trees! (Desert **Poplar**) Not many, but enough for us to think we might find water.

Everyone started talking and morale picked up.

Charles sent teams in all directions to dig.

Hours later, we returned to camp sweating and exhausted.

NO WATER!

The roots of a desert poplar can be very, very long.

Water was somewhere, but it was too deep in the desert for us to find.

Suleiman was worried and spoke with Charles.

'This is serious; the camels are weak and will start to die. They must have water.

The alarming news spread quickly through the camp.

You have probably already realised that camels are awesome creatures; they are brave, strong, and sometimes a bit grumpy but, more worryingly, they don't let you know when things are wrong. They keep going until they suddenly stop, and it's all too late.

Time for some more maths and CHECK THE WATER AGAIN!

Mark dipped a stick into each container, carefully measuring and recording how much water we had. We checked and double checked. Our lives depended on these calculations being right. When Charles was sure he had all the correct information, he announced his plan to the whole crossing team.

'We need to restrict our water to one litre (one water bottle) during the day'… lots of groans and shaking of heads.

'It will be the same for everybody; there will be NO exceptions to this rule. A little more water will be available for cooking.'

This announcement caused angry protests from some team members. Charles was furious and could not believe the wimpy and rather pathetic reaction of some.

He raised his voice and shouted, 'By reducing how much water we each drink, it means we can give all of our camels a five-litre bucket of salty water – putting it simply – if the camels die, it won't be long before WE ALL DIE.'

That's pretty easy to understand, or at least you would think so. The Chinese team was visibly frightened and our camel-handlers became even more quiet and withdrawn.

If Charles, Rupert and Mark were frightened, they didn't show it and neither did I. Instead, we focused our energies on working together. Charles needed to get everyone on side. He asked Zhang (Chinese interpreter) to help share the water out.

Rupert and Zhang organised and controlled the division of the precious water.

This was a survival situation for camels and humans!

The mood of the teams changed; fear and tempers flared. Our camels too were frightened; they jostled and bellowed, desperate to be first in line for the buckets of water. 📷 Rupert and Zhang did their best to ensure each camel received one bucket.

Although helpful and quite possibly saving their lives, it would be like you being given an eggcup full of water, then being told to pick up your rucksack and continue walking in the blistering heat for another day.

I want to let you into a SECRET. I have not shared this with anyone else…

I knew if things got really bad, we had more water.

Everyone, apart from me, had forgotten the intravenous fluid that was in the emergency medical pack.

Three litres. It doesn't sound like much, but it could be the difference between making it out of the desert or NOT.

I decided not to mention it.

My plan, if things got really bad, was that I'd give the emergency fluid to the strongest and most able team member – Rupert, and send him out of the desert to organise the rescue.

Sven Hedin, in 1895, did something similar to save his camel-handlers, but hopefully, unlike Hedin, Rupert would not bring water back in his boots!!!!

CHAPTER 35

Urgent Resupply
Barney to the Rescue!

Drastic action was needed. Charles shouted, 'Unload the camel sacks and get rid of anything that's not essential. We must reduce the loads.'

Rupert and Mark radioed the support team.

'We need an urgent resupply. Can you travel north into the desert? We will turn south. With luck and some spot-on navigating, we should meet up.' Later we found out that the support team were terrified about getting stuck in the sand again. When the vehicles were fully loaded with containers of water, they were too heavy and sank deep into the sand. Barney's support team took everything they possibly could out of the vehicles to lighten them. This gave them the best chance of getting the precious water to us. For the last five weeks we had walked from west to east across the desert, so it felt odd when we altered our direction and turned south. Like a needle in a haystack, the hope of locating the support team was surely a slim chance.

Moving slowly in the intense heat, we meandered lethargically through the hot, soft sand. The sun beat down on us and despite wearing sunglasses it became almost impossible to see anything, other than the shimmering heat haze and the glare of the sun.

For several boiling hot days, we had survived on one litre of water each, that's the equivalent of three cans of fizzy drink. It was during this time that I was so affected by being thirsty, that still to this day when I turn on a tap to fill a kettle, or just get a drink, I remember the desert and being desperately thirsty. Holding my water bottle gazing at it, I wanted to guzzle it down in one go. I stopped myself and took only a tiny sip, as we still didn't know if we would find the support team.

Rupert and Mark forged ahead. 📷

As they approached the area where we hoped the vehicle (Bella) might get to, they divided up in an attempt to search a larger area of the desert, desperately scanning the horizon with binoculars. After what seemed like an eternity a shout went up from Rupert.

'I can see something flashing.'

He raised his binoculars and peered again. 'I think it's Krishna flashing a bright light. YES, it is. He's using a mirror catching the sun and looking straight at me with his binoculars.'

A bright light flashed and glinted across the dunes. Waving and smiling, we headed towards Krishna. What a relief to see the support vehicles parked up in the dunes; a beacon of hope, defiantly flying a huge Union Jack. (Up the right way this time.)

Barney and his team were smiling and rightly so, they had SAVED US and the expedition! We hugged and thanked our team mates, not thinking too much about what would have happened if they didn't get to us.

We loaded up with fresh water and gave another bucket of salty water to each of the camels. Reluctantly, we left our friends, turned north and headed back up into the desert to pick up the original route. The support team watched and waved, started their engines and headed south out of the desert back to the Silk Road. Our change in direction was to have an unexpected but exciting consequence.

CHAPTER 36

Broken Pottery
A New Navigator and
Who's Eaten My Biscuit?

Twisting and turning through the dunes to get back to our original course, we started seeing something odd: bits of broken pottery scattered on the desert floor. 📷 What I haven't told you is that we were on the edge of one of the ancient sites discovered a hundred years ago by the archaeologist, Sir Aurel Stein.

Charles and Mark stopped to see if they could find anything, while Rupert and I carried on. We started seeing more and more pieces of pottery.

Rupert pointed.

Poking out of the sand were several wooden pillars and lots of **rattan woven walls** half buried in the sand. 📷 Charles had often spoken about the possibility of finding an ancient site, so perhaps this was it.

Rupert contacted Charles on the radio to share the news.

'I think we've found something.'

Even Rupert sounded excited.

We gazed around, taking it all in. It was an incredibly lucky find because if we had walked on the other side of the dunes, we'd have gone straight past.

Charles and Mr Guo called everyone together.

We needed to treat the area with great respect.

Excitedly Charles gave another one of his speeches! 'We will take photos, sketch the area, and record all the map coordinates so that one day archaeologists can come back to this exact spot and learn about the civilisation that lived here many thousands of years ago.'

The year before we left for China, we were very lucky to visit the British Museum where a team of archaeologists spoke to us about the people that lived in the desert and the artefacts that had been found by previous explorers a hundred years ago. At the meeting we all thought exciting, but didn't really expect to find anything. We were wrong!

It felt odd to walk through the ancient village, almost as if we shouldn't be there. Outside the ruins of huts were old rubbish tips. It was here that, without really looking, I found and picked up an orange glass bead. I held it in my hand, rolled it around and gazed at it.

How old was it?

Who had it belonged to?

Was it part of a necklace or used as money?

Whatever it was, it was beautiful and incredibly old, and I didn't feel comfortable having it. Happily, I handed it over to Charles who carefully wrapped up a few small pieces of pottery, some old fruit stones and the glass bead. 📷 At the end of the expedition, all artefacts and information would be handed over to Chinese archaeologists.

The next day, Charles wanted to make a recording for the BBC Radio diary and continue mapping the area with Mark. Paul busily sketched.

Rupert radioed the support group for Mr Guo who needed to speak to the Chinese team.

This was my chance to be the NAVIGATOR.

The idea of the 'Camel Doc,' a woman, navigating and leading the way caused the Uyghurs and Chinese to snigger and look worried.

I was annoyed by their attitude but not surprised.

There's no difference between following a man or a woman as long as both know how to use a compass!

This would not have been be a good time to get everyone lost and have the men all say, 'I told you so.'

The pressure was on... I like to think that my route was kinder to our camels. I also took time to explain to the Uyghurs how the compass worked. They were interested but surprised a woman knew such things. I shared my knowledge and as far as they were concerned, more importantly, I shared my food.

We carried extra rations to snack on during the day: biscuits, chocolate bars (melted and frozen several times) and hard-boiled sweets, to keep up energy levels and boost morale. Like when you are collected from school and if you're lucky your mum or dad might bring you a snack for the walk home.

WHY?

1. Because you're hungry.

2. It cheers you up.

Exactly the same reasons we had snacks.

Towards the end of the day, one of the Uyghurs, Lucien, liked to sing. It was never the most tuneful of songs and continued until we stopped for the evening. Mark came up with a cunning plan. When Lucien started to sing, he walked beside him and chatted, then offered him a hard-boiled sweet.

Who can resist?

It's not easy to suck a sweet and sing, so desert peace was restored.

Another treat that our camels had become very fond of was BISCUITS! A sponsor who couldn't give money donated a huge load of biscuits. Only one complaint. There were no chocolate ones; in the heat of the desert this was probably just as well. We had to be careful at lunch breaks when perhaps, for extra comfort, you leant up against a seated camel. If you were not sharing, but nibbling a biscuit and chatting to your friends, LOOK OUT! 📷 Our camels had developed quite a taste for those delicious round snacks. Before you knew it, your biscuit DISAPPEARED!

Camels have prehensile lips, which means they can cleverly hold things with them. When they wanted, they could be very gentle and carefully extract a biscuit from the fingers of someone who was not paying attention, causing much laughter and shouting of, 'WHO STOLE MY BISCUIT?'

CHAPTER 37

Starting to get Cold
Who Has the Best Beard?

The weather had been changing gradually for the last few weeks. It's now freezing at night and in the early morning. Our amazing camels are perfectly designed to survive extremes of temperature; their furry coats keep them snuggly and warm in the cold but also cool in the heat.

To keep us warm we put on brightly coloured puffy coats, woolly hats and gloves, stoked up the fire and huddled together. 📷

Here's my rather strange nightly routine.

Sitting by the fire, the first thing I try to do is thaw out a frozen block of wet material. WET WIPES!

At some stage in your life, you will probably have had them used on you! Perhaps as a baby during nappy changes or when you get covered in CHOCOLATE! Basically, anytime you can't get water to clean yourself. So, this was me attempting a sort of wash. I peeled frozen sheets of wet wipes off and used them to clean my face. Then, if it wasn't frozen solid, I applied moisturiser and sun block. Using a mirror, I looked at my face, usually groaned, and then applied some lipstick, making the men laugh when I said, 'One has to keep up appearances. I am having supper with thirteen guys every night.'

The men pretended they didn't need the mirror, saying it was a girly thing to keep looking in the mirror. But secretly, each of them borrowed it to check how their beards were growing, pulling and tugging at their facial hair in an effort to improve its growth.

A competition was being held...

Who's got the best beard? So far, Mark was winning.

The men were beginning to look a bit wild and dishevelled, with dry, cracked and sore lips.

'Not wearing your lipstick,' I would say with a laugh. I frequently encouraged them to put on lip balm and apply suncream. They chose not to listen and consequently got blisters and sores on their faces. Using moisturiser and lipstick was not about looking good but, more importantly, about protecting skin from the harsh desert sun. 📷

At eighteen, when I joined the army, a wise old RSM (Regimental Sergeant Major) – a very strict lady, a bit shouty and scary, said to my squad, 'Anyone can be uncomfortable.'

In her own way she was trying to help us; being uncomfortable is easy, but to be comfortable requires planning and engaging your brain.

Life in the desert was tough enough without making it worse for yourself.

Now that it was colder, I noticed how the camels snuggled up next to each other. I never actually saw a camel asleep. They always appeared to be gazing up into the inky blue/black night sky. Perhaps, like me, they were waiting to see a shooting star.

Using headtorches or sometimes a candle and occasionally the light of the full moon, we wrote in our diaries.

I don't remember who it was, perhaps a teacher, said to me, 'If you ever do anything unusual, keep a diary.'

I know it sounds a bit boring, but it helps you to remember and it's something to do. Also, you can let off steam, saying things in your diary you wouldn't say out loud!!

Like GET ME OUT OF HERE!

Sitting by the fire or from the warmth of our sleeping bags we wrote in our diaries. One of the Uyghurs, Emir, sat with a battered precious journal recording his thoughts and observations. I wonder how different his story was to ours. He also liked to write poetry, and was given the nickname 'The Poet.' Every night we slept out under the stars. We prepared our own sleeping area by scooping out a body-length trench, laying a mat in and then a sleeping bag.

Next, you surround your area with equipment and personal belongings creating a little home for yourself. Most nights, I gazed up into the dark sky, only happy when I spotted a shooting star. There was no light pollution in the desert. Millions of sparkling stars beamed out for all to see. It wasn't long before a bright silvery white light flashed across the night sky leaving a trail of star dust.

Quickly, I made a wish.

What do you think I wished for?

1. Lots of water to drink.

2. To get safely across the desert.

3. A hot bath or shower!

Other curious rituals:

The batteries that powered the radio transmitters, satellite navigation, cameras, etc, were collected up and divided between us. We then put them in our sleeping bags!

I can hear you say, 'That's a bit weird!'

There was a good reason; we were trying to save their power. In extreme cold, keeping your batteries warm helps stop them losing energy.

It's funny what you can get used to.

Drinking swimming pool water and salty water, sandy food, and now batteries in your sleeping bag!

We slept like guardsmen, lying to attention with batteries down each side. If you weren't careful when you rolled over, a battery jabbed into your ribs. Despite the batteries, by 2100hrs (9 pm) most nights we were sleeping like babies only to be woken at 05.30 by the sound of electronic bleeping from Rupert's watch. One of us got the fire going while the rest of the British team stayed in their sleeping bags until they knew the water was boiling. Occasionally Mark (Kipper) needed a little more encouragement to get moving. If it was your birthday, you had tea brought to you in your sleeping bag. Sadly, it wasn't my birthday while we were in the desert.

The British team then set about trying to wake the rest of the camp.

Just a reminder here of who and what we had to get moving every morning. Also, don't forget, it's DARK and FREEZING COLD!

1. The Chinese Team X 4

2. The Uyghur camel-handlers X 6

3. Bactrian camels X 30

4. Breakfast for 14 people.

5. Breakfast for 30 camels.

6. Load up 20 water containers = 10 camels

7. Load up 40 camel sacks = 20 camels

CHAPTER 38

Frozen Ropes, Icy Sleeping Bags and Tiny Paw Prints

Overnight, the water containers started to freeze up and the ropes froze solid. 📷 Loading up in the morning became even harder, shredding the hands of those trying to tie on loads. Wearing big gloves made it difficult to undo the ropes, but bare hands quickly got cold and injured.

Something needed to change. Rupert took charge. 'Can we please try NOT to leave the ropes in big heaps. It's virtually impossible to undo them in the morning when they are frozen together in giant knots.'

Rupert demonstrated how to untie and leave the ropes, laying them carefully out on the desert floor ready for the next day. It did speed things up.

At about the same time every night a sandstorm swept over the desert. Luckily, we were usually asleep. In the morning, little heaps of sand all over camp started moving. From beneath the mounds, people appeared, sat up, rubbed their eyes, shook off sand and laughed at each other. Rupert looked the funniest, like a giant panda except with little white eyes popping out.

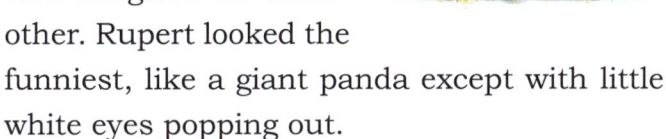

He slept with his head out of his sleeping bag so consequently got completely covered in sand.

Now that it was really cold, I started using an extra outer layer over my sleeping bag called a **bivvy bag**. It's like a huge waterproof, windproof bag with a hood that you put everything inside, sleeping bag, rucksack, boots etc. Warm yourself by the fire, then run to your sleeping bag and jump inside. I wriggled around inside the giant bag and took off my clothes. When I did this, Rupert said I sounded like a giant packet of crisps. (Rupert was always thinking of food!) The bivvy bag was made of Gore-Tex: crinkly and quite noisy. It protected me from all weathers and strangely I felt safe inside it. I slept in tracksuit bottoms and a long-sleeved cotton t-shirt, NO socks! With a woolly hat pulled firmly on, I must have looked funny! I kept my clothes inside the sleeping bag, partly as a pillow and also to keep them warm. I zipped up the bivvy bag. Just my nose poked out; I 'attempted' to stop the sand getting in (IMPOSSIBLE) and keep creepy crawlies out!

Although we never actually saw any insects or reptiles the Uyghurs told stories of giant snakes and scorpions! Eeeek, I did not want them in my sleeping bag!

Occasionally we came across tracks left in the sand by snakes or other animals, I was taking no chances and zipped up my bag.

Things you don't want in your sleeping bag:

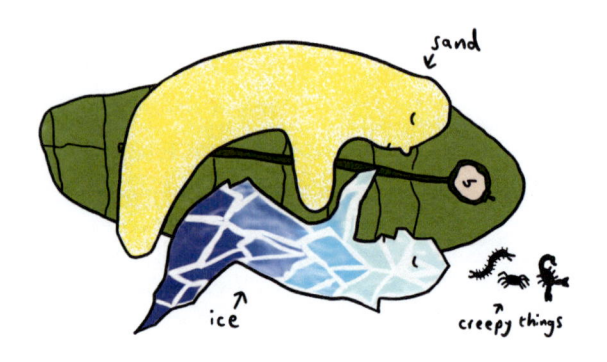

sand

ice

creepy things

In the morning it was a reverse of the night before. Wriggle around to get dressed in your sleeping bag. The only problem was that now the bivvy bag had ICE on the outside and the INSIDE!!!!! Ice crystals showered down as you moved. I guess it's one way to wake up! There was definitely no opportunity for a lie in!

You had to get up...QUICKLY.

Dramatically, I unzipped, leapt out and ran across the sand to grab a place by the fire. Huddled together, we cupped our hands around hot drinks.

We placed our frozen boots as close as we dared into the flames, thawing them out, before reluctantly easing our sore feet back into them.

One morning, I made an interesting discovery: lots of tiny paw prints around my sleeping bag.

I asked Rupert, Mark and Charles 'Have you been visited by little desert creatures?' When we looked, we found paw prints all over the camp!

Here's another secret, and I am hoping you don't do this at home.

At night we ate BISCUITS in our sleeping bags! This is probably a good time to talk about 'brushing teeth.' Honestly, I brushed my teeth every night and every morning by dipping my sandy tooth brush into a water bottle. (Not sure what the boys did!!!)

As we munched on our BISCUITS, crumbs spilt onto the desert floor. Without realising, we had attracted quite a following of desert gerbils and **jerboas**.

The rodents, like our camels, have adapted to life in the desert. They are nocturnal creatures, coming out when it's dark to forage for food. That's why we hadn't seen them. I imagined our little furry desert friends scurrying around, telling all their pals they had found an amazing supply of food and water.

It's possible that some had hitched a ride in the camel sacks, excited by the prospect of an adventure with lots of food and water. (Little rodents only need tiny amounts to drink; a drip from one of our water containers would completely soak them).

I wonder what story the five-toed pygmy jerboa would tell as she hopped and zigzagged her way across the desert. They too were on a very, very big adventure.

The desert gerbils and their friends were too clever for us; we only ever saw their paw prints.

The crossing team was now:

Fourteen humans

Thirty camels

Hundreds of rodents: gerbils, desert rats, etc.

All 'attempting' to make the world's first crossing of the Taklamakan.

Sounds like a PIXAR movie.

Who would be the stars?

I agree... definitely the CAMELS and the GERBILS!

CHAPTER 39

Fizzy Drinks and Ice Cubes

Spare a thought for our poor camels; those shiny water containers were frozen solid. It would be like having two giant ice cubes strapped either side of your tummy!

Not very nice when you are cold, but refreshing when later in the day you are hot.

By midday, things had warmed up and the ice started to melt. Sloshing water and bits of ice chinked in the containers. It was a new sort of torment for the thirsty.

I called it 'G&T time.' (Or lemonade and ice time!)

It was TORTURE!

CHINK, CHINK, CHINK, SLOSH, SLOSH, SLOSH went the sound of ice and water!

EEEEEEHHHH help!! I AM... Soooooo thirsty!!!

The last of the thawed water was divided up.

Some team members drank their water quickly, almost expecting to get more, but they didn't. Rupert controlled the rations strictly.

I allowed myself one tiny sip every half hour! For the next twenty-nine minutes all I thought about was WATER!!

The resupply was thankfully close.

WATER and REST; it's not much to ask for.

Strange things happen when it's really hot and you are very thirsty you start to see things that aren't there!

Called a **mirage**; and caused by layers of air being at different temperatures which bends the light causing refraction and the appearance of what looks like water. One that I saw looked like a huge lake. I knew it wasn't there, but I still thought that looks cool I will dive in for a swim.

NOPE

Depressingly, as we walked towards it, it vanished!

However, on this day we were all seeing the same thing and thinking secretly to ourselves, 'It must be another mirage?' It really looked like water. As we got closer... hooray, it didn't disappear, we almost FELL IN.

A narrow stream of icy water, the Andir River, from the **Kunlun Mountains** in the south, flowed out into the desert and then disappeared deep into the sand.

A river was marked on the map but usually only flowed during the summer. We were incredibly lucky to find it running in the autumn.

Our camels stopped, bent their heads down and sucked in what must have been the most delicious cool mountain water they had ever tasted. 📷 North of Yawatongguz, in a small oasis village, we rested for two days. The army calls this R and R (rest and recuperation), and we certainly needed it. Busily, we prepared for the final three hundred miles! Still three hundred miles to go! 📷 The camels had lost a lot of weight. We needed them to rest and eat!

Guess what?

They didn't need any encouragement. They are awesome at eating and drinking.

Over two days their floppy, sad-looking humps started to plump up and look happier.

I think I should give you some information about camel humps. Contrary to popular belief, their humps DO NOT hold water, but store fat which, when they are hungry, can be used for energy. (Forgive me if you already knew that!)

So, if you ever see a camel with sagging droopy humps, you know they are hungry, thirsty and unhappy. Quickly get them food and water, and don't get too close!

Barney **bartered** and traded with local people who kindly supplied sixty eggs and fifty traditional naans cooked in outside **clay ovens**.

This was seriously exciting: something different to eat. We divided the fresh bread and eggs between the teams.

Paul was happy with his sketches and left the crossing team.

Keith's blisters had healed, so he re-joined us.

CHAPTER 40

Ancient Hunters Boring Jokes and Falling Out

Back in the desert, we crossed an ancient dry river bed and found some unusual black stones. Even tired eyes spotted something different on the desert floor.

Lao Zhao, the scientist, explained his theory on where he thought the stones came from and how they ended up in the desert. He suggested they were left by prehistoric man maybe ten thousand years ago on a hunting trip. The stone was flint from the Kun Lun Mountains. Ancient hunters carried large flint stones and chipped off small pieces when they needed to make arrow heads, knives or scraping devices. We had great respect for

Lao Zhao and loved hearing his stories. He knew more about the desert than anyone. He told us that, thousands of years ago, this area was very different; there was a large lake with rivers and a dense forest of poplar trees. (The wood we had been burning.) Wild animals: boar, deer, rabbits, and wild camels, including the sadly now extinct **Caspian tiger**, roamed the area. The flints were left behind from a long-ago hunting trip.'

Lao Zhao's stories were a happy distraction from the now boring daily slog. Mark was also a brilliant storyteller. He made up stories and walked along the camel train telling us the latest instalment. Sometimes, his stories went on for days, as we begged him to tell us more.

Keith cheered us up with tales of the support team's adventures. He also strangely wanted to know about **Cockney rhyming slang**. Now this did give us a lot of laughs because although we knew some words like:

Apples and pears = stairs
Bubble bath = laugh

Dustbin lids = kids!

Dog and bone = phone.

That was about it. So, unbeknown to Keith, we just made words up and he wrote it all carefully in his diary. Laughing, sharing stories and just having fun together was vital as we tried to keep our spirits up.

But the truth was, camels and humans were exhausted and weary of the routine. Let's be honest, I wasn't bored with the desert, but I was bored with some of the stuff that was going on. The same BORING jokes repeated most days, many of which were about women and yes, I am a woman, so I did feel a little ganged up on and, the truth was, the jokes were not even funny! SORRY, I am ranting a bit, but these things happen when people are living and working in extreme conditions.

You learn a lot about each other, but mostly you learn about yourself!

Over the last two months we had all changed our behaviour, SOME MORE THAN OTHERS! It was a gradual change that I think many had not realised had happened.

For example, the lunch stop had been quite civilised.

NOT anymore!!

The sack that contained the food was just emptied out onto the desert floor, and everyone scrabbled around in the dust and snatched what they wanted. 📷 I don't think the dinner ladies at school would be very happy if you tipped your pack lunch on the floor. I struggled with the chaos of lunch and chose to wait until the scrum had finished. Mark noticed, picked up some biscuits and, with a smile, gave them to me.

'Come on, Doc,'

I thanked him and said,

'Take a look around. What has happened to us? We are behaving like wild animals, fighting over food.' IT WAS TRUE.

The expedition had affected us physically and mentally. Rupert and I fell out during loading. I admit, I was not at my best in the morning and snapped when Rupert made another joke about women. I shouted at him. Rupert, always larger than life, bouncy and smiley, would have been happier if I had punched him.

A verbal attack wounded him more; he retreated from my company. The friendship we had forged over the previous months was surely stronger than one angry exchange at a time when neither of us was at our best. We avoided each other for a few days. This was no time for sulking.

How long can you be angry with a big, smiling, friendly, dependable RUPERT? It turns out, not very long... we hugged, laughed and were friends again.

Charles lost it with Rupert and Mark. They had formed a close bond, a brotherhood, that at times excluded all other team members. I was happy with that, but Charles was upset, feeling left out of the 'boy gang.'

Chatting at the front of the camel train for hours and lost in their own 'boy world', they sometimes didn't concentrate and took a wrong turn.

Charles shouted at them for messing around. 'I am going to separate you. You're too cliquey, excluding others from your conversations and, worse still, leading us all the wrong way.'

Rupert and Mark stood in front of him like naughty school boys, looking down and kicking the sand, shoulders shaking, trying not to giggle. They could hold it no longer and exploded with laughter. By this time everyone was laughing including Charles.

But he was right. When the lead scout was on his own, concentrating, our twisting, meandering route through the desert definitely improved.

The Uyghurs quietly, without fuss, got on with the job, never really complaining, although they did need a lot of encouragement to get up in the morning. As you may remember, they were not keen to move before sunrise.

YAWNING

The Chinese team was tired and beginning to show signs of rebellion. They had separated themselves from the other teams, and huddled in a small group whispering. Mark who spoke Mandarin told us they were not happy. It was clear they'd had enough of following Charles!

The camels too were exhausted and weakened by weight loss. Apart from during the water crisis when tempers frayed, they appeared to be good friends, only occasionally fighting with each other at feeding time – normal behaviour for hungry camels. Oh, and the other time SPITTING they loved to play up was during loading. They made such a fuss, bucking, bellowing and spitting their breakfast out!

I guess they hoped we'd give up trying to load them. However, their cunning plan backfired.

Seeing a camel without a load, some team members thought, 'Oh, my legs hurt, my back hurts, everything hurts. I don't want to walk. I shall ride a camel.'

Luckily for the camels, those team members that liked to ride had also lost weight. If they did ride, it was not for long. Sitting on top of a camel in the autumn meant they got very cold. The daytime temperature often didn't get above freezing.

Lao Zhao made us laugh with his observation.

'When I walk, my legs hurt. When I ride a camel my bottom hurts!'

TIRED, EXHAUSTED AND FED UP.
An ominous feeling hung over the expedition.

CHAPTER 41

Bad Things Start to Happen

Something was very wrong.

The camel-handlers were upset, praying, and saying, 'This is a bad omen.' Suleiman the lead camel-handler, was too upset to even speak to Charles, so he sent Kirim to explain. Through interpreters, Kirim said, 'In the night for a few hours there were thirty-one camels.'

We didn't understand.

'What do you mean, we had thirty-one camels?'

It turned out the thirty male camels were not thirty male camels. One of them was female, and sadly she had a **miscarriage** during the night.

The 'Camel Doc' was called into action.

Sensitive to her situation and standing in the half light of the breaking dawn, I gazed into her eyes, carefully stroking her side. It's not widely known but very rarely and usually, when no humans are about, camels can and do, cry. We shed a private tear unnoticed by the rest of the now busy camp.

What a terrible way to discover I was not the only female on the trip. The only good thing was that at least now I had a friend.

The miscarriage upset us all. A baby camel had been born too early because its mother was on this treacherous expedition. It's not easy telling male and female camels apart, so you must forgive us for believing we had thirty male camels. If the little camel had survived, Rupert was ready to carry it around on his shoulders. What an amazing story that would have been, but sadly a calf born at six months had no chance of survival. (Normal **gestation** for a camel is thirteen months).

As I stroked the side of my new friend, I thought she needs a proper name and asked Suleiman to suggest an Uyghur name. This idea seemed to cheer him up as he smiled and said, 'Fatima.' Suleiman's ten-year-old granddaughter was called Fatima, he said she was brave, strong, beautiful and occasionally just little bit cheeky. Charles suggested I walked with Fatima. It sounds strange but I needed female company even if it was a camel. Fatima's head hung low, she knew exactly what she had lost. I tried to comfort her, speaking softly as I led her through the dunes. Stroking her side, I shared all sorts of secrets, my hopes and dreams and how I missed my family and friends.

We spent hours together.

Just me and Fatima. She plodded along quietly, appearing to listen to my stories. I remembered I had half a packet of biscuits in my rucksack... for emergencies, this was definitely an emergency, I pulled them out and gave them all to Fatima. We definitely had a bond, even a friendship – a sort of sisterhood. Not many people can say they had a camel for a friend.

It was Mark's birthday so we tried to cheer ourselves up by celebrating. Somehow, I made a cake out of... can you guess what? Melted chocolate bars and digestive biscuits!

We sang 'Happy Birthday' and shared the cake.

The main birthday surprise was a giant shiny green watermelon, saved from the last resupply. With great excitement and anticipation, the juicy melon was meticulously sliced into equal pieces and shared around.

Holding the succulent watermelon with two hands, I walked carefully across the desert, gazing longingly at the red flesh as juice dripped onto the hot sand. Smiling, I patted Fatima, took one bite and held out my hand. 'Come on,' I waved it again under her nose. She looked at me. 'YES, I want you to have it. Quickly, before I change my mind.'

She needed no further encouragement and gently removed the sweet, juicy melon from my palm. We both knew it wouldn't cure her heartache but for a moment its mouth-watering sweetness transported us both to a happier place.

CHAPTER 42

Final Resupply and the Last Chocolate!

Approaching the village of Tatalong, we carefully navigated around the edges of huge paddy fields, trying hard not to fall into the intricate and ancient irrigation system. Farmers in wide-brimmed hats stooped as they planted rice deep into the muddy water. They looked up, surprised to see us.

What a sight we must have been:

Thirty weary camels and fourteen weather-beaten humans slowly walking out of the desert and into their village.

The support team had set up camp on the edge of the village. Charles' huge yellow map hung on the side of one of the vehicles.

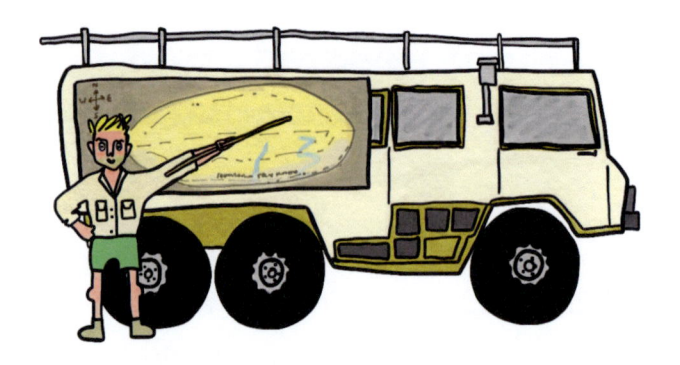

Everyone gathered around.

'This is the final part of our journey.' He pointed with the stick he used to walk with. 'Here's where we started.' He traced a line across the map. 'We have come a long, long way. What we have achieved is nothing short of a miracle. We've nearly made it across!!' (He pointed at the end.) 'But there can be NO relaxing. We must stay focused.'

Finally, the last phase of the expedition!

HOPEFULLY… just thirteen days to go!

It was like that end of term feeling.

We worked busily together on the final calculations of how much food and water we needed to get us to the END!

One of our sponsors didn't give money, but instead gave us something even more valuable: huge amounts of CHOCOLATE BARS!

You are probably thinking it's a bit silly having lots of chocolate in a hot, hot desert, surely it melted! Yes, it did every day it melted, then every night it was frozen solid. By the time we got to eat the bars they were very odd shapes... but luckily, they still tasted delicious.

My favourite job was dividing up the CHOCOLATE bars! Charles decided at the beginning of the expedition that I was the only person he could trust with this very important job!!!!

Believe me... I guarded that chocolate with my life.

I knew where it was and who was going near it.

People were desperate and temptation could strike at any moment! The chocolate was safe with me!

Our chocolate supply was running low. We had just about enough to get us to the end. Sadly, we only had a few bars of everyone's favourite. I put all the bars we had left in a camel sack, shook them up and then asked each person, without looking, to draw out thirteen bars. Each of us had to decide if we ate a bar a day or munched them all at once. I always saved my bar until the middle of the afternoon when my energy levels and mood could drop, it was something to look forward to. If I was feeling ok, I saved it until the next day, it was always good to know you had an emergency chocolate bar at the bottom of your rucksack even if it was squashed. Rupert cheered when he pulled out four of our favourite nutty bars. When he realised I had none, he smiled and swapped me two of his – the sign of a true friend. Did I ever give myself more CHOCOLATE than anyone else? It was tempting but honestly, I NEVER cheated on my teammates. We were in this together.

We checked and rechecked our supplies and loaded up for the last time.

Keith stayed with the support team and the crossing party went back to fourteen people.

Flags were up and flapping in the wind as Charles gave his final rallying speech... like your headteacher at assembly saying, 'YOU can pass your exams!'

'We can do this,' said Charles. 'The end is in sight. Let's get out there and bite the dune for one last time.'

('BITE the dune' was another of Charles' funny sayings. It meant 'Get up and over those sand dunes!')

I would like to say we departed with a wave and a spring in our step, however, it was more of a backwards glance and a limp, as into the desert we went FOR ONE LAST TIME.

CHAPTER 43

'I Should Not Have Had Those Noodles!'

A cold wind blew.

We had encountered many sandstorms over the previous weeks, usually at night when we were snuggled up in our sleeping bags.

This storm looked different.

Ominously, the sky darkened and the sun was blocked out by sand, quickly turning day into night. 📷 Time to wrap a scarf around your face and put some goggles on.

Scarves up and ski goggles down, we attempted to battle on against the increasing wind. Suleiman shouted to Charles.

The message, although whipped away by the wind was clear – we needed to STOP.

'It's too dangerous to continue. We will get separated and lost.' Suleiman gave instructions to sit the camels in a large circle.

What a brilliant idea. We sat and sheltered inside the protective ring of big hairy camels.

Although designed to withstand sandstorms, even they are unable to see which way to go in the darkness of a black storm, known to the Uyghurs as a **Kara-Buran**.

It was safer to stop and wait for the storm to pass.

The wind howled and hissed as sand was pummelled into us. The temperature dropped. Peering through the whirling sand and darkness, I looked for Fatima and snuggled up next to her. I wrapped my favourite brightly-coloured spotty scarf round my face and pulled down my hat. It was impossible to talk over the roaring wind. The only thing to do was to close your eyes and dream. The storm raged for several hours. When the wind dropped we stood up, shook off the sand and moved back onto the trail. Ahead of us... guess what... More sand mountains...yaaaaaaaay!

The sand was fine and deep. Once again we were wading through it. I remembered the day I bought my boots in a camping shop in Devon.

The shop owner normally supplied people with boots that kept them dry on boggy Dartmoor, so was surprised when I asked for 'Boots that are high up my leg to stop sand going down inside.'

When you stood on the slopes of a dune, the sand was above your knees. It felt as if the desert was sucking you in, sapping every ounce of the little energy you had left.

Charles, Rupert, Mark and I pulled, pushed, waved and yelled encouragement to our camels and everyone else as up and over the dunes we went. BITE THE DUNE!!!

One evening, there was nearly a disaster. It was late. Rupert, Mark and the Uyghurs were digging by the light of an oil lamp. Desperate for water, the camels paced around and got too close to the edge of the waterhole. The sand collapsed in, nearly trapping the men below. Thankfully, Abdul (BP) reacted quickly, shooed the thirsty camels back and pulled the men out. After months of extreme exertion, silly mistakes were happening more and more often.

You might remember that I didn't suffer from the giant frying pan illness (Squits). Until now my health had been fine. UNFORTUNATELY, I had been tempted by some wonderful noodles at the last resupply, made by a kind Uyghur lady. How could I say no?

OHHHH HOW I WISH I HAD!

It's never fun being ill, but it's especially bad when you are the team medic. While you are being sick, you are thinking, this is not good. Who is going to look after me?

Next morning, Rupert and Charles were concerned.

'How are you, Camel Doc?'

'Diarrhoea, vomiting and abdo pain (tummy ache); other than that, I am OK.'

I tried to smile and make light of my discomfort. There was no hiding the fact that I was not well.

Rupert was the support medic, which meant if I was ill, Rupert was going to look after me!

He was excited. 'Do you need a **drip (intravenous fluid)**? I can do it, really I can. Let me have a go. PLEASE.'

Rupert was desperate to have a go! I didn't doubt his ability, but I wasn't quite ready to let him stick needles in my arm!

'No, thank you, Rupert, not yet. I will let you know if I need your expert help.'

Rupert was disappointed and Charles wanted me to ride a camel!!!!!!

I think you can imagine how that conversation went.

Of course, I REFUSED!!!!

I had walked every inch of the way and was not about to give up now. Rupert had also walked all the way, he understood my determination and quietly encouraged me with, 'You can do it mate.' I valued his support and continued to walk, albeit slowly.

Over the next few days my 'Dashing to the Dunes' reduced and gradually I improved.

CHAPTER 44

Disaster Strikes

Sand mountains and NO WATER!

Sound familiar?

The camels were thirsty and wandering off searching for tamarisk bushes and trying to find moisture from dried up twigs! It was whilst doing this that one camel got into trouble.

This next bit is sad, so be careful when you read it.

Some grownups have said I shouldn't tell you this part of the story, but I think you want the truth and will understand. Let me make it quite clear; we didn't want this to happen and it upset all of us.

Late at night, snuggled up in my sleeping bag, writing my diary by the light of the moon, I heard a shout from the Uyghur camp. Charles and Rupert went to investigate.

Then a call I couldn't ignore. 'CAMEL DOC!'

What was it this time?

Another knife wound or more blisters?

NO, it was much worse, and I couldn't help, although I really wanted to.

A camel had fallen on a steep dune, dislocated its neck, and was unable to get up. Suleiman led our desperate efforts to help the animal, pulling and pushing, but it was hopeless. The camel was surprisingly calm and didn't appear to be in pain. At least, I hoped that was the case.

Unable to move, we made him as comfortable as we could. Something had to be done.

We couldn't stand by and watch it suffer.

Now, in my role as the 'Camel Doc', I spoke with Charles and Suleiman. Charles suggested, 'Can you give the camel an injection to put it out of its misery?' I don't know what Charles thought I had in the medical box, but certainly I did not have enough medication to humanely kill such a huge animal. Suleiman suggested we wait until the morning, hoping that one of two things happened:

1. There was a miracle and in the morning the camel was up and running around.

2. More likely... that the camel died in the night.

I don't think any of us really thought the poor camel would be trotting around the next morning, but we had to hope.

Silently, we went back to our sleeping bags.

The Uyghurs stayed with the camel and prayed.

Dawn broke and for the first time everyone was up, but the camp was eerily quiet.

An unpleasant judgement lay ahead.

Charles and Suleiman quickly made the decision.

The injured camel had to be killed.

We could not leave it to suffer or wait to see what happened. I had no wish to watch the poor creature meet its end, so busied myself helping feed and calm the other camels. Charles, Rupert and Mark helped the camel-handlers move the camel to face Mecca. What happened next was in keeping with the Islamic faith. Suleiman prayed into the camel's ear, asking for forgiveness for what he was about to do, and for the camel to go to a better place, which was certainly going to happen. He knew exactly what to do and swiftly put the camel out of its misery.

Anger, frustration and fear spread rapidly through the camp. Charles called everyone together.

'None of us wanted this to happen. We are all sad. The camels are the heroes of this expedition. Losing one so close to the finish is very upsetting, but this is a survival situation and tough decisions have to be made.' The Chinese team blamed Charles for the death of the camel. I suppose they thought, it was Charles idea to cross the desert, and he gave the final order for the poor camel to be put out of its misery… So it was his fault!

Charles had a meeting with Mr Guo.

'Please reassure your men. I had no choice. If we are going to get out of here alive, we have to keep the expedition moving.'

The Uyghurs were used to making tough choices. Living on the edge of the desert, they faced life and death decisions daily. They would not let the camel's death be a waste. The fleece kept them warm at night and the meat provided much-needed nourishment.

That night, around the camp fire, not all team members felt able to eat the food that was now available.

Rupert tried to make everyone laugh by asking, 'Who wants a camel kebab?!' 📷

SORRY, I know that's not very nice – army humour again! Rupert was doing his best to cheer us up.

As team medic, I also advised on nutrition and encouraged all team members to consider the extra protein. Emir cooked the meat and politely offered some to ME first! The Uyghurs smiled at me. Remember it's a survival situation, I reminded myself and took a bite. It tasted fine; no different to any other red meat you might eat. We were hungry and needed to build our strength back up.

The Chinese team refused, saying, 'It is like eating your best friend.'

Upset, frightened and fearing for their lives, our Chinese friends believed we would stop at nothing to succeed.

Camels and humans were subdued and spent a restless night.

As we settled down under the stars, I heard an unfamiliar sound. High in the night sky, a 'V' shape of large birds flew over.

In the light of the moon the birds glowed a magical silvery white as they honked noisily to each other, probably surprised to see camels and people so far into the desert. Today whenever I see or hear swans I think back to that incredible and unexpected sight.

The next day, as usual, Rupert was out front leading through the never-ending dunes that now formed huge walls of sand. He stopped, looked at something in the sand, and then shouted to Charles.

'Our Chinese friends are not going to like this. It will be another bad omen.' Everyone stood around and gazed at a beautiful, but sadly, frozen white swan.

Lao Zhao said that he thought it was a **Bewick swan** flying south from Arctic Russia to spend the winter in Southern China. The flock stopped to rest and this poor swan got too cold.

THREE BAD OMENS and still a hundred miles to go!

CHAPTER 45

Will We Make It? Exploding Congee and Goodbye Biscuits!

Everyone had been affected by the events of recent days and, just to add to the misery, it was now cold all of the time. We Brits are obsessed with the weather, monitoring it and talking about it all the time. Remember, we started in late summer and it was now late autumn going into winter. Rupert informed everyone that the day-time temperature was -5°C and at night it was dropping to –25°C!

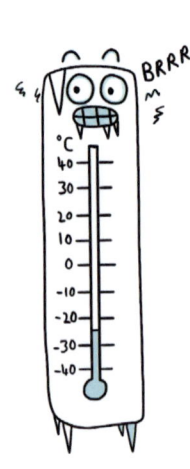

I think you would agree that's a bit chilly!

The expedition had taken on a whole new challenge. Everything was frozen solid and remained frozen. Even the cooking oil was frozen and had to be thawed out by the fire before it could be poured into the famous giant frying pan.

The sand mountains were now sand walls: sheer vertical barriers fifty to a hundred metres high. If you weren't careful, the sand avalanched down on top of you. There was no choice; we had to walk around them. 📷 The tangled dunes continued relentlessly, worse than anything we had experienced before, yet this, we had thought, was supposed to be the flat area of the desert!

Charles called a meeting and spread his gigantic map out on the desert floor. Leaders of all the teams knelt in the sand around the maps with Mr Guo, Suleiman and Zhang to interpret for the Uyghurs and Mark to interpret for the British and the Chinese. Also present was the scientist, Lao Zhao, who looked carefully at the map, which was really a large piece of yellow paper with the words 'sand dunes' marked on it. 📷 Lao Zhao confirmed everyone's fear; there was no flat area of the desert. He told us the map was made years ago when someone flew over the desert in a small plane, looked out of the window every now and then, and wrote 'sand dune' or flat area! So, it wasn't much help!

Our friendly scientist also said, 'I tried to tell you at the beginning, but no one was listening.'

The Chinese team insisted Charles changed the route. Reluctant to alter his original path, he paced around, scratched his head but finally agreed. The less challenging terrain to the south, that had been visible and tempting us for some time, gave the expedition a chance of making it out alive and completing the crossing.

'It's the first ascent of Everest, not the route taken that is remembered,' said Mark, trying to make Charles feel better.

Our camels were now so weak that when breaking through the top of a steep dune, if they stumbled and sank to their knees, they were unable to get back up.

If this happened, we had to be quick. We ran to them, cut the rope and dragged and pulled with all our might. Everything had to be done superfast to keep the momentum going, ensuring the rest of the camel train continued to move up and over the dunes to safety. The camels unable to stand were unloaded, stood up and moved on to a flat area to be reloaded. This was a long and tedious task, draining everyone's energy. The loads were not heavier. The camels had become weaker. Some of the stronger camels angrily threw off their sacks. Perhaps letting us know they could not go on like this for much longer. Our progress was painfully slow

After eight hours of walking, Rupert's GPS depressingly informed us we had only managed six miles and to make matters worse, NO WATER and NO WOOD had been found.

Time for another headteacher talk from Charles.

'I know we are ALL exhausted. Our camels are trembling and weak. We must lighten their loads again. Get rid of anything that is not essential.'

Camel sacks were emptied onto the desert floor.

Rupert and Zhang took charge.

The Chinese team dramatically set fire to their excess kit and food, they had mountains of food, far more than was needed, I guess they were worried about getting lost and being hungry. They stood around the blazing fire with long faces.

Flames leapt into the air and smoke billowed as tins of congee (a rice-like porridge with bits of vegetables) exploded! Even Rupert, who ate anything, was glad to see the back of the congee.

A thick black smoke swirled around and then crept off silently into the desert.

We decided to bury the ration packs and equipment we didn't need. Charles said, 'May be in a hundred years, archaeologists will dig up our kit and remember our great expedition.'

'Let's hope it's not like previous expeditions, when only the leader survives!' said Mark which, strangely, made us laugh! (Desert madness?)

The Uyghurs watched and must have thought us odd to waste precious food and equipment. When they thought no one was looking, they tried to rescue things. Rupert found BP stuffing some food back into a camel sack. BP smiled at him and rubbed his tummy. The giant tough man admired by the Uyghurs didn't have the heart to make BP throw the food back. He put a finger to his lips and whispered, 'Our secret.'

Rather than waste the grain, we gave our camels an extra meal and, best of all, the thing they loved more than anything: handfuls of our favourite biscuits.

As you can imagine, the hungry camels made short work of the heaps.

Goodbye biscuits!

CHAPTER 46

Kirim Goes Missing

Could things get any worse?

YES.

Suleiman frantically shouted to Charles, 'Kirim is missing.'

'What do you mean, he's missing?'

Mark interpreted. 'He went about two hours ago, probably looking for wood. Now it's dark; they are worried he won't find his way back. They think he's going to die.'

'OK, let's not panic. Get out two emergency **flares** and see if we can guide him back.'

Rupert climbed the highest dune and set the first flare off. It lit up the night sky and hung above our camp for what seemed like several minutes, creating an eerie white light by which we could all see each other. We shouted and called out, but there was no sign of him.

'Let one more flare off, Rupert, and let's just hope and pray he sees this one,' said Charles.

Up it went. Desperately, we peered into the darkness.

At the edge of the light cast by the last flare, I spotted a tiny figure.

'There he is, and it looks like he's carrying something.'

Kirim received a hero's welcome as he staggered back into camp pulling behind him a large bundle of firewood.

We hugged him and each other, relieved that we were safely back together again.

Kirim had walked a further two miles searching for wood.

He beamed with pride as a fire was lit and the Uyghurs, Chinese and British teams huddled together sharing the heat and each other's company.

During early dawn, as the sun battled to rise over the mountains to the south, Charles, Rupert, Mark and I sat together high up on a dune.

Wearing our puffy red and purple jackets and sipping hot sweet tea, we stared at the twisted knots of dunes that lay between us and the edge of the desert. 📷 Charles pointed into the distance. 'The end is in sight but I am afraid, as you can see, no flat area. We are just going to have to get on with it and continue to bite the dune. There is NO easy way out.'

BITE THE DUNE! I've had enough of biting the dune. We've been doing that for weeks and weeks!!!

No point in getting emotional about it; the flat area didn't exist! Sitting in that nice warm office in London six months ago, planning our trip, somehow we had convinced ourselves that the last bit of the desert was going to be flat.

WRONG!!!!

We sat in silence contemplating the final push.

📷 You will see I don't look very happy.

📷

Go to website thecameldoc.com for a real life photo

CHAPTER 47

End in Sight

Each camel train was led by an Uyghur who, patiently and unquestioningly, followed the route set by Charles. The four camel trains also had people walking at the back and encouraging from the sides. I walked with the first camel train led by Kirim and the lead camel, Chumba, whose name means big and strong; he was like the boss of the camels. We set the route and speed for the others to follow. It had been the same every day for the last few months, but today things changed. There was a split.

We headed on the previously agreed slightly altered route away from the sand mountains but still crossing the widest point.

Rupert and Charles led the way, followed by Kirim. Everyone else was supposed to follow. Mark and I looked back and saw that some of the camel trains had gone in a very different direction. Mark used his handheld radio to contact Charles.

'We've got a problem, boss. The other camel trains seem to be turning even further south towards the edge of the desert.'

Charles was furious. 'They are heading out of the desert. This is not the route we agreed.' He tried to contact Mr Guo but he had turned his radio off.

'What do they think they are doing? Risking lives; the expedition will fail. Why are they doing this?' Charles shouted angrily into the desert.

Rupert grinned. 'It's a race to the finish.' Mark and I agreed, great idea; anything that meant we could get out of the desert sooner.

'No,' said Charles. 'We started together and we will finish together. A Joint British–Chinese Expedition.

It's ONE TEAM of British, Chinese, Uyghurs and camels.

That is how we will conquer the Taklamakan.'

Charles was right and we knew it; the race was off.

We contemplated our next move. The breakaway group was part of our team. They were our friends and, although their actions annoyed us, we had no wish to see them perish in the desert. Their fitness and map-reading skills were dubious. They stood little chance without us.

Something else rather crucial they had overlooked – our camels were carrying most of the water!

Reluctantly, we altered our route AGAIN and went in search of Mr Guo and the others. 📷 All those years/months ago when Charles looked at a map of the world and thought I am going to try and cross the Taklamakan Desert, his choice of route was based on nothing more scientific than drawing a straight line from west to east across the middle.

It was several hours before the two teams were reunited. Charles had time to think, calm down and decide how best to address the problem.

Both teams were angry, blaming each other.

Charles and Mr Guo spoke privately. The situation needed cool-headed diplomacy from both sides.

Before he left the desert with dysentery, Richard spoke to Charles about the potential for a diplomatic incident – British and Chinese teams falling out. Richard gave Charles advice on how to patch things up when the inevitable happened. Don't forget, we were guests of the Chinese nation. The British and Chinese governments wanted the expedition to be a success. Crossing the desert was important, but more important was the friendship and trade between the two nations.

We needed a solution that kept everybody happy.

The two leaders talked.

When they finally re-joined us, they were smiling and embracing.

They had found a way forward that both agreed on. Charles spoke to the teams.

'Together we are strong. Together we have travelled across the desert, adventurers, and friends, and TOGETHER we will finish it. I agree with Mr Guo that we can change our route again, but we must finish at the correct place so that we can claim the world's first lateral crossing.'

At last – a route to the END.

CHAPTER 48

Chopsticks, Forks and Socks

Firewood and water always boosted team happiness.

We built a huge communal fire and sat closely together sharing stories, food and, for the first time in weeks, laughing and smiling.

Lao Zhao, sitting on a water container by the fire, reached into the front pocket of his orange **cagoule** and produced a carefully tied bundle. Delicately, he unwrapped his prized possessions. Mark interpreted. Lao Zhao explained that he found the stones many weeks ago in the Mazartagh mountains and now he wished to present the largest one to the 'Camel Doc' who, he said, 'was like the great British Prime Minster,

Mrs Thatcher and she too will be known as the 'Iron Lady of China.'

He said I had shown 'great courage and determination.' He placed a sparkling crystal into my hand.

I was honoured, embarrassed and a bit shocked to be compared to Mrs Thatcher!

He gave smaller crystals to each of the men, praising in particular, 'The Mad General' as he called Charles for his leadership and determination to follow his dream.

Smiling proudly, we thanked Lao Zhao for sharing his knowledge of the desert, for his sense of humour, which could always be relied upon, and for his uncanny ability to tame the flame-throwing cooker and, of course, his culinary expertise.

Over the weeks of our adventure, I had observed many curious things.

This was the strangest:

At the start of the expedition the Chinese ate their supper using traditional chopsticks and we used knives and forks. Nothing odd there, just as you'd expect.

However, now at the end of the expedition, we were using chopsticks and the Chinese were using forks!

How very odd. What did it mean?

Perhaps it symbolised that finally we had accepted each other's cultures and embraced our different ways of life.

Whatever it meant, I was just happy we were working together and enjoying each other's company.

The camels too were making history.

No camel before had walked the entire West–East crossing of the Taklamakan and certainly my friend, Fatima, was the first female camel ever to cross the desert. Proving, I believe, beyond question, that a female camel is as resilient and courageous as any male!

Even though we were close to finishing, the daily routines continued. My camel clinic was now easier. The camels knew what was going on and happily lined up waiting to see me. They never gave me any problems: no spitting or kicking and not even any camel breakfast!

At last, we had well-behaved camels!

Apart from weight loss and being exhausted they were healthy and their wounds had healed. We humans were not doing so well.

Sniffing and coughing, some had toothache, some sore and chapped hands and most of us were limping. I checked on everyone and handed out various tablets to help ease pains or treat infections. Sometimes all that was needed was a smile, a pat on the shoulder and a few words of encouragement.

You know when you are tired after a really busy term at school, you sometimes start making silly mistakes? You might cross the road without care or forget your cycle helmet – not because you want to live dangerously but because you are tired and just not thinking straight.

Well, that started happening to us.

Charles cut his finger trying to fix one of the BBC recording devices. Emir received a headbutt from a camel (camels, you have learnt, are not always nice to humans, especially if you are pulling on their ropes).

Emir's head and Charles' finger needed stitching up. These incidents always happened at night, making the whole thing trickier to deal with. Thank goodness for my headtorch. 📷 Our cuts and scratches, like the camel's injuries, healed well. A dry, hot desert is a good environment for healing wounds.

DO EXPLORERS WEAR SOCKS?

Answer coming up...

I am sure most explorers wear socks, however... Rupert and I didn't wear SOCKS. That's right. **NO SOCKS** for the whole crossing!

It's not quite as ridiculous as it sounds. Let me explain why we made such a decision.

As a nurse in the army, I had looked after **veterans** (old soldiers). These men were known as **The Desert Rats** (not the fluffy creatures with long tails but another army nickname). An old gentleman who remembered his time in the Sahara Desert during World War Two, told me, 'We never wore socks; it reduced friction and helped prevent blisters.'

He explained that when sand got into your boots and then into your socks it made them a bit like a piece of sandpaper that rubbed and scratched your feet!

I had remembered his advice and both Rupert and I decided to give it a go! Our feet had survived well until, annoyingly, with less than fifty miles to go, I started getting my first blisters.

WHY?

I sat by the fire with my boots off and stared at them.

Carefully, I examined them and noticed that the laces were really fat. I rolled them in my fingers – they were full of sand! Perhaps sand was in the lining of my boots? Taking my trusty Swiss Army penknife (it goes everywhere with me) I cut into the lining, tipped my boot up and, hey presto, out came a long trickle of fine sand.

No wonder I was getting blisters, it was like wearing shoes that were too small. Mystery solved.

Which leads me on to another mystery. Back in chapter four I asked:

HOW MANY PAIRS OF SOCKS AND UNDERWEAR do you need to pack for an expedition?

Here are MY answers. I say 'MY' answers as I don't know what the boys packed!

Perhaps I should ask Rupert, but I am not sure we want to hear the answer. It might be too revolting!!

1. SOCKS = ten pairs. I left five pairs with the support team. (I wore socks in the evening.)

2. UNDERWEAR = fourteen pairs (enough for two weeks!!!!!).

Before you start feeling faint about wearing the same underwear for weeks... we did get a chance to wash stuff at the resupply.

The last night in the desert was by far the coldest. It was definitely chilly because even

Rupert was wearing all his arctic gear. The whole camp slept badly, perhaps because it was cold, or possibly because it was our final night together. The next day the special friendship we shared would change forever. The Uyghurs who still didn't trust our map reading skills after following us for fifty-nine days, didn't believe we were going to get out of the desert that day. Rupert and I tried hard to convince them. 'You really don't need to eat the Sven Hedin bread rolls. Honestly, we will get fresh food very soon.' Remember, those bread rolls had been in a camel sack from the beginning of the expedition! And I don't think they were fresh then. 📷 The Uyghurs carried on eating. The bread was rock hard, but they were taking no chances!

If you look at the photo you can see BP trying to bite through one. I am surprised he didn't break another tooth! 📷

The final desert breakfast was completed. The camels were loaded up for the last time.

Charles gathered everyone around and thanked each of us. We had all played a part in helping make his dream come true. He then asked that we spend a quiet moment.

We stood solemnly together, heads bowed, as prayers of thanks were said from three different faiths: Muslim, Buddhist and Christian. 📷

Charles recited the Gaelic blessing with Mark translating into Chinese and Zhang translating to Uyghur.

> **A GAELIC BLESSING**
>
> May the road rise to meet you.
> May the wind be always at your back.
> May the sun shine warm
> upon your face and
> the rain fall soft upon your fields,
> & until we meet again.
> May God hold you in the
> hollow of his hand.

The special friendship that the desert had allowed us to develop would soon change.

A sadness passed between us.

'Cheer up, everyone.'

Said Charles 'We are HEROES. The world is waiting for us.'

The flags were brought out for the last time. Charles suggested to Mr Guo (who was no longer the rotund Mr Guo) that they swap flags as a sign of friendship between our countries.

Mr Guo walked at the front of the camel train just ahead of Chumba holding the Union Jack and Charles walked beside him waving the Chinese flag. In the distance we started to see people climbing up sand dunes and waving. My feelings were a mixture of excitement, relief and a strange sadness that our expedition was ending. You might get the same feeling when you finish junior school and move up to senior school, happy to have finished and be starting your holiday, but also sad not to see your friends and have the routine of school life.

We walked slowly trying to take it all in, wanting to make the magic of the desert and our expedition last just a bit longer. People came into the desert to greet us, one of the first was Keith the photographer, he was determined not to miss a thing and busily took photos as we inched closer to the end. Film crews appeared on the top of dunes, they waved and shouted to us. Smiling to each other we proudly made our way towards the edge of the desert at Luobuzhuang. We were greeted by cheering crowds, more film crews, the world press and our support teams.

It was an odd feeling. One of those happy and sad moments!

When you climb to the top of a mountain it's very dramatic and, if you are lucky, you get a spectacular view, but crossing a desert... well, you just get to the other side!

The flags were planted on the top of a dune.

All members of the crossing and support teams were filmed and photographed from every possible angle.

Colourful garlands were hung around our necks and champagne popped. 📷 We hugged and congratulated each other; we had completed the world's first ever lateral crossing of the infamous Taklamakan Desert.

Not to be ignored, the desert had one last, very rare and unusual surprise for us. A flurry of snow filled the air and turned the desert white.

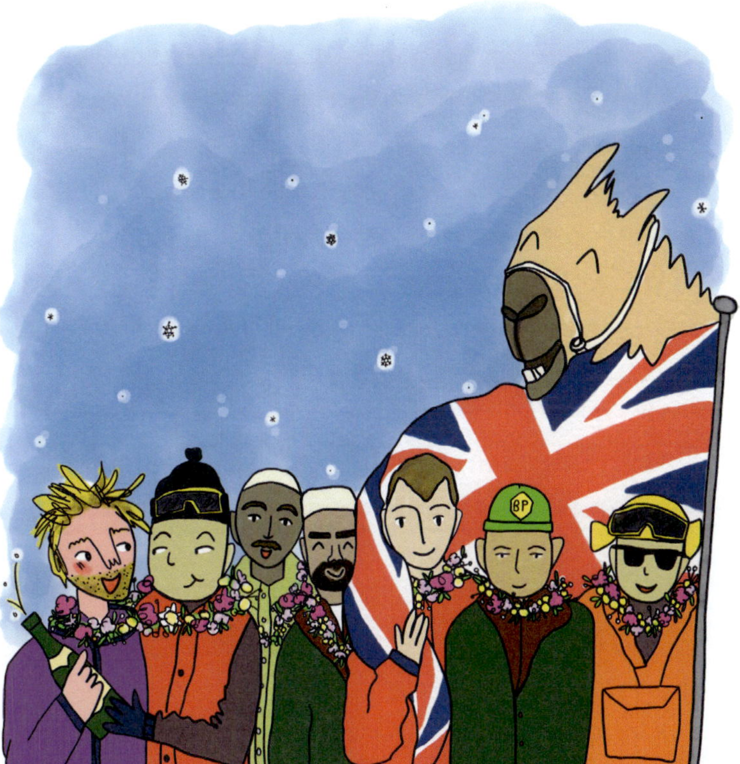

BP

CHAPTER 49

The Official of Hot Water

Smartly dressed officials presented us and our camels with sashes to wear. The gold and red silk was decorated with Chinese writing that celebrated the Chinese, Uyghur and British heroes who had conquered the infamous desert. Together, we had disproved the legend,

'You go in but you don't come out.'

We were living proof that, if treated with respect, military planning and ok, I admit it – a certain amount of luck – the desert could be crossed.

With our sashes proudly blowing in the cold wind and flags flying, we paraded through the streets of **Ruoquiang**. 📷 The streets were lined with hundreds of people of all ages. A colourful and noisy welcome of fireworks, cheering, and music greeted us.

Walking along in a bit of a daze, busily shaking hands, I took time to say hello to some smiling children who had been given a day off school to see 'the desert heroes.'

We were introduced to lots of important people, but no one more important than the 'OFFICIAL OF HOT WATER.'

STOP, this was someone I needed to meet. With my interpreter helping, I explained that regrettably I had not washed for... sixty days!!!!!!! EEEEEEEKKKK

I hoped I didn't smell!

What do you think about not washing for the whole of the summer holidays?

REVOLTING!

It wasn't like being in a busy polluted city with no showering for sixty days... now that would be SMELLY. The desert was clean, dry and the sand sort of washed you. Maybe I was kidding myself – that I didn't smell! Perhaps the people we met were thinking, 'What is that whiff?' And they were just too polite to say anything!

Strangely, I was quite excited about the thought of being able to wash. The boss of hot water promised he would do everything possible to ensure later that day we MIGHT get a HOT shower! In 1993 hot water and indeed running water was a luxury in many areas of the Xinjiang region of China.

Once through the busy streets, we led the camels into the quiet, walled compound of a guest house and gave them a well-earned feast.

We met two new camel-handlers: Suleiman's brother and nephew, both camel farmers. It was their job to guide our camels back home to Hotan, four hundred miles away!

Our poor old camels still had a long way to go, but at least this time there would be no heavy loads.

Their journey would be leisurely, safe and with…

NO SAND DUNES!

The Official of Hot Water lived up to his name. That afternoon I had my first shower for sixty days!!!

Unfortunately, it was not quite like the one I had been dreaming of.

Little children peered in, and a sewage drain ran through the middle but, true to his word, the water was HOT!

My sun tan washed off!!!

After not washing for so long my skin didn't really enjoy the hot water and soap and became dry and itchy, I had to use lots of moisturising cream, but at least I was now clean!

Remember my emergency pack at the bottom of my rucksack, I could now open it and put on clean white…

The expedition was over!

The first night out of the desert we stayed in a guest house.

I had a little room on my own. I didn't like it; I felt trapped, lonely and strangely unsafe. The mattress on the bed was thin, which I know sounds a funny complaint from someone who had slept on the sand for sixty nights.

Paul (the artist) found three more thin mattresses.

REMEMBER,

I haven't slept in a bed for sixty nights!

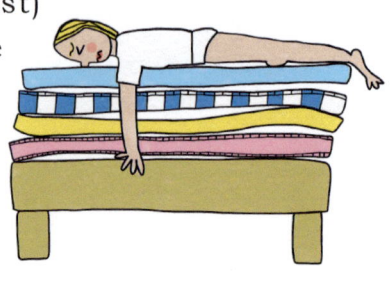

I haven't slept inside for sixty days…

I missed the stars and sounds of the desert.

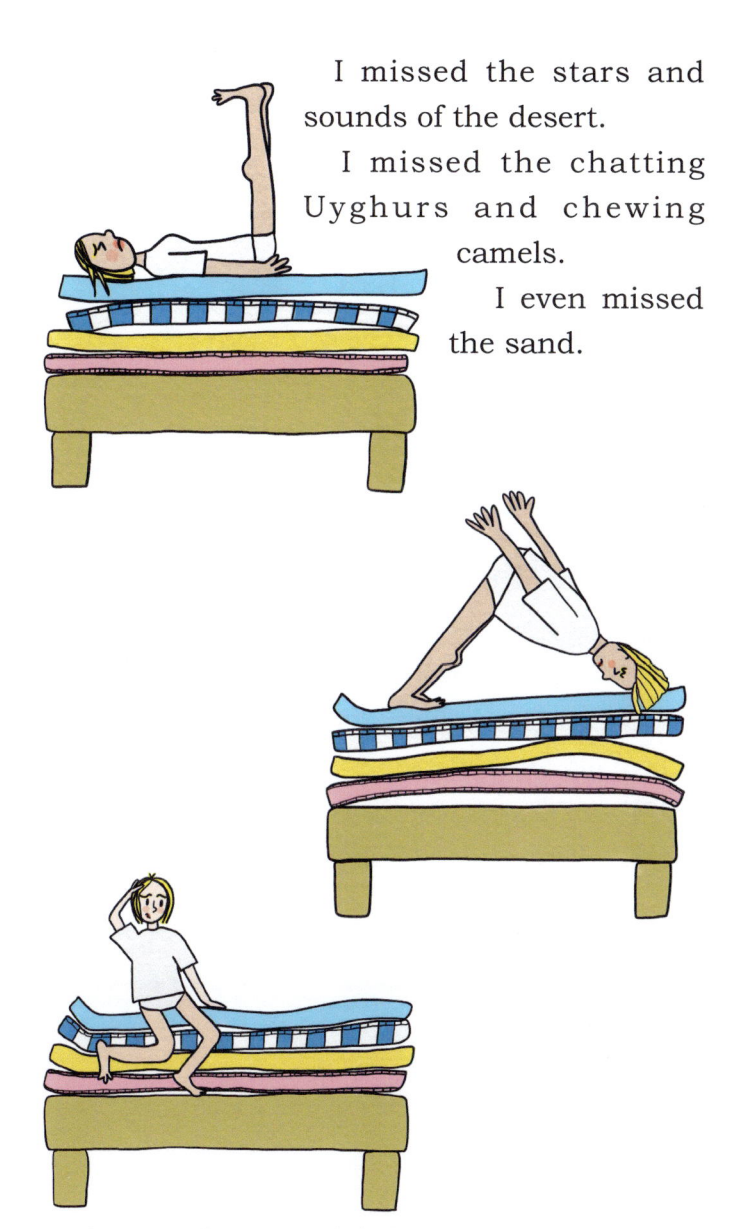

I missed the chatting Uyghurs and chewing camels.

I even missed the sand.

Guess what?... I didn't sleep very well.

CHAPTER 50

A Message from The Queen! and Goodbye Camels

In the compound, a huge fire was ceremoniously lit and the night sky burst into life with more fireworks. Music boomed out as important people came to join the party.

A magnificent banquet was held in our honour. Long tables were laden with local delicacies and glasses were raised as everyone toasted and celebrated the conquering heroes of the desert. Ancient Chinese military leaders, some reputed to have been on the **Long March** of 1935, smart in their uniforms, lined up, bowing their heads to pay tribute and meet the teams. They especially wanted to be introduced to the two people who walked the whole way. Rupert, who towered over the venerable old men, bowed and shook their hands. But the person they most wanted to meet was a woman –

'The Camel Doc.' ME!

They praised us both enthusiastically, raising their glasses and shouting 'ganbei' (which means 'dry cup') – swallowing the drink (baijiu) in one go!

Spotting the long queue waiting to see me, Mark came to my rescue.

While at university in Beijing, he had learnt about many Chinese customs and traditions, including knowledge of food, drink and etiquette. (HOW TO BEHAVE!)

Quietly, Mark whispered, 'This stuff is like fire water. It's extremely strong alcohol and you have a really long line of generals, dignitaries and admirers all wanting to toast you. Tradition and etiquette is to drink it down in one go! The secret is, don't let them refill your glass to the top otherwise, although you walked across the Taklamakan, you will find you won't be able to walk back to the guest house tonight!' I laughed, and together we made sure my glass was not filled up too much.

Mark interpreted as each general gave a little speech. He was very excited when one of the generals insisted he should put his glass lower than mine when we chinked glasses. 'Golly, Doc, that's a serious honour and it's caused quite a stir – he considers you have higher status than him.'

I only wish this historic evening had been filmed for you to see. After the banquet, we went back to where we were happiest – outside, around the fire. 📷

Together for one last time, the Uyghurs, Chinese and British, smiling, dancing, laughing and hugging each other.

Despite our different cultures and religions, over the last few months we had developed a unique friendship. We were clinging onto the last few hours before we returned to our very different worlds.

Up early the next day, we sorted through our kit and gave quite a few things to our Uyghur friends. We packed up the vehicles and drove north to Korla and then on to **Urumqi**, before flying to the capital, Beijing, then onto Hong Kong and finally home to the UK.

Did we look any different? Most of us were a bit weather-beaten. Some team members had lost weight.

One of the biggest changes was Francis.

Do you remember at the start of the expedition, his wife had said he didn't laugh much anymore and always wore boring old suits? Well, I hoped she was ready for the new Francis. His neatly trimmed hair was now so long that Rupert teased him, saying perhaps he should start plaiting it. The boring clothes were gone and in their place were brightly coloured local materials complete with baggy trousers and a funny floppy hat!!! Francis had gone native and was loving it! Certainly, we would take home a more relaxed and colourful Francis. His wife and children would be happy and the city of London, where he worked, was in for a shock!

We heard news of 'Little Bean' – remember he was really ill and had to leave the desert for emergency treatment. He spent several weeks in a hospital but was now well enough to chat to us on a phone. Remember also Esa Polta the original lead camel-handler who fell off a camel, hurt his leg, and then upset us all by saying he wanted to go home to die? Well, he was in fact alive and well. He had become a local hero and a bit of a celebrity telling stories of his desert adventures.

Expeditions like ours change people; they make you think differently about life and what's important. I suppose it's rather obvious that being thirsty would play a big part in a desert adventure, but nearly thirty years later whenever I turn a tap on, I remember how thirsty we were, clean water gushes out and I think how lucky I am.

Suleiman, Emir, Kirim, Lucien and Abdul (BP) came with us to the large industrial city of Urumqi where we attended more state banquets and celebrations. And for them the biggest excitement was that, for the first time in their lives, they would fly in a plane home to their families in **Kashgar**.

Keith dashed around taking photos of everyone.

Without saying it, we were saying goodbye.

We just didn't want to admit it. 📷

The teams lined up for final photos, smiling and even hugging some of our amazing camels.

(Not all of them enjoyed such close human contact!)

Chumba had a special photo taken with Mark who had won the competition for the best beard. 📷

Charles thanked everyone personally, then proudly he read aloud from a **telegram** that had arrived that morning.

It was a message from Buckingham Palace and the QUEEN of ENGLAND who was 'Delighted' to hear the news that the Joint British–Chinese Taklamakan Desert Crossing had been a success. She sent, on behalf of the Duke of Edinburgh, herself and the nation, her heartfelt congratulations to all those who took part.

Once I tried to explain to the Uyghurs where I was from by drawing a map showing China and various other countries. I pointed to a tiny island thousands of miles away over land and sea. I explained: 'This is England, part of Great Britain.' The Uyghurs laughed at such a small country. I was not sure they understood. Then I remembered my emergency £5 note (no idea how I thought it was going to help in an emergency!).

I showed them the picture of the Queen now they understood.

The Uyghurs cheered.

They knew all about the Queen of England and were very fond of her. We smiled, patted each other on the back and hugged, proud that the Queen of England was saying well done to us.

News of our success was travelling around the world.

Some months after my return to London, I was very lucky to be **presented** to Princess Margaret.

I will never forget her saying to me, 'My sister and I followed your expedition across the Taklamakan. We had our maps out and plotted your journey across.'

I smiled politely and then, like the Uyghurs, the penny dropped... your sister... Oh, you mean THE QUEEN!!!

I still have the vision in my head of the Queen and her sister studying a map spread out on a huge polished table at Buckingham Palace. Perhaps they had a small golden camel that moved as they tracked our progress!

We loaded up our trusty camels for the very last time.

The bags were no longer bulging with equipment, and there were no huge sacks of rice.

All they had to carry was food for themselves and a few items belonging to the Uyghurs.

It was strange saying goodbye to them.

We had been through so much together.

The camels didn't look bothered. I imagine they were glad to see the back of us and our silly ideas.

I found Fatima, my bestie for the last few weeks and thanked her for listening to me. I don't know if she realised that we had BOTH made history.

Both achieved world firsts...

First female camel and first woman to walk the thousand miles from West to East across the TAKLAMAKAN.

The rusty metal gates of the compound were pushed open. Chumba led our brave camels out... finally we were all on our way home but I had one last thing to do before we left.

I presented BP with my desert boots, 'Sixty days without washing, you are welcome to them.'

Everyone laughed, but not BP. He gazed into my eyes, beaming with happiness. He now had his 'Ella yukshee' (Very beautiful) boots! Keith photographed this very special moment.

Do you think BP wears them with or without SOCKS or does he keep them on a shelf and tell stories about his adventures in the desert?

One day I will go back to visit our Uyghur and Chinese friends and find those boots. I wonder what other adventures they have been on...

A Big Thank You from the Camel Doc

CONGRATULATIONS!

You've crossed the desert and finished the book. I really hope you enjoyed it.

How do you feel? Exhausted? Relieved? Thirsty?

Perhaps you're excited to see what adventures you could have in the world.

Not everyone who reads this story is going to pack up their rucksack and head to the nearest desert.

However, I hope it might make you think... YOU could do something unusual or just something others don't believe you can.

Perhaps you want to walk to the North Pole or be an astronaut and visit Mars, work in cybertechnology, help people by becoming a doctor or nurse, teach people by becoming an awesome teacher, become a scientist and study viruses and invent new vaccines, go to the

Olympics or cycle in the Tour de France, design incredible new houses for us to live in or build them, invent new GREEN ways to generate power, appear on the *Great British Bake Off*, or become a golf ball diver. Yes, that job does exist. You go diving to retrieve golf balls that end up in lakes!

I think you get what I am trying to say... Follow your dreams... who knows what you will be able to do?

Just in case you are thinking, 'Oh, I couldn't do that,' here are a few things that happened to me when I was young that prove you CAN.

1. My grandma (nana) said I would never be a nurse! Apparently, I cried a lot when my brother was run over. He was fine but broke his leg and spent the whole of the summer holidays in hospital. I visited every day! (What a good sister!!!) I think it's ok to be upset when your brother's hurt. Grandmas can occasionally get things wrong, but not often! I was a nurse for more than thirty years and can honestly say I loved every day.

2. If you are reading this, then my book has been published... yipeeeeeee... and I will

have proved a few people wrong! It took me five attempts to pass 'O' level English (GCSE). I only got through thanks to the help of my uncle, an English teacher! I passed various 'O' Levels and 'A' Levels but without 'O' level English, my life would have been very, very different. All those years ago no one talked much about dyslexia. Everyone just said I was bad at spelling. With determination, the right help and support, dyslexia WILL NOT hold you back.

3. I went on a Girl Guide camp when I was twelve... I hated it. I missed my family. I didn't fit in. I didn't get on with the other girls. I didn't like the silly rules and, most of all, I hated the toilets!!! I packed my rucksack and walked home thinking, 'This camping lark is not for me!'

Not the most promising of starts for someone who, eighteen years later, walked across a desert and was given a GOLD MEDAL by the Scientific Exploration Society as the Woman of Achievement for 1994.

If you have enjoyed my story and would like to learn more, please visit the website www.thecameldoc.com

Also, if you have questions for me, just email cameldoc1@googlemail.com.

I would love to hear from you.

If you would like me to visit your school, ask your teacher to contact me. I'd be very happy to meet you and your friends to talk about desert adventures and of course CAMELS!

Glossary

Amoebic dysentery. Occurs in countries with poor hygiene. Caused by a parasite that lives in food or water.

Sir Aurel Stein. Hungarian-born British explorer, archaeologist, geologist and surveyor. He discovered a ruined Buddhist site in the Taklamakan and the world's oldest printed text one thousand six hundred years old (the Diamond Sutra) discovered in the Mogao Caves. You can find out more about these amazing and very important discoveries at the British Library.

Bactrian camel. Their Scientific name is CAMELUS BACTRIANUS. A large group of camels is called a flock or a caravan. They have two humps and a long thick shaggy coat to protect them from the cold, beautiful long eyelashes and special nostrils that can close to keep out sand. They have huge flat footpads that stop them sinking into the sand.

Bartered. The trading of goods or services between people without using money. Bartering has been used throughout history, for example famous artists like Picasso, Van Gogh, Matisse and Dali paid for their food and drink by quick sketches or paintings; today those artworks sell for millions!

Bear Grylls OBE. Former British Army Officer, adventurer, author, TV presenter and Chief Scout.

Bewick swan. Smaller than mute and whooper swans. They can be seen in the UK; they spend their winters here as it's warmer than Siberia where they breed. They also take holidays in Japan and Southern China. (These were the swans we must have seen on their way to somewhere a bit warmer.)

Bivvy bag. The word bivvy is shortened from bivouac, meaning a temporary shelter made by soldiers or mountaineers. A thin waterproof cover that goes over your sleeping bag, it replaces the need for a tent.

Brackish water. Is salty water but not as salty as sea water. Not good for humans to drink but mostly ok for camels.

British Ambassador. An important person of the highest diplomatic rank. Based in a foreign country they protect and look after citizens of the UK who need help. They also try to establish good relations and trade with other countries.

CCCC (Camel crossing for children's cancer) We raised money to support the charity founded in the memory of Leonora, the daughter of Lord and Lady Romsey.

Cagoule. A lightweight, thigh length, thin, hooded waterproof jacket, quite often orange, with a big pocket in the front.

Caspian tiger. Sadly, extinct since the 1970 due to being hunted and changes to its environment caused by humans. Records show that this huge tiger could measure up to 3m in body length + another one metre of tail! Genetically, it may be linked to the Siberian tiger.

Chapans. An Uyghur word for a long cloak or coat worn over clothes.

Chewing the cud. When camels eat, their heads are down and they are vulnerable (can't see much) so they eat quickly. Later, with their heads up, they regurgitate their food and give it a good chew to get moisture and goodness out.

Clay oven. A hollow dome-shaped structure made of clay usually used by the whole village to produce flat breads. Through a hole in the top, they stick the flat discs of dough to the hot clay walls of the oven. The bread is delicious!

Cockney rhyming slang. Thought to date back to early 19th century from the East End of London. It's a sort of coded language possibly to hide the true meaning of discussions from the listening ears of the first ever police force. (The Bow Street Runners.)

Cotton. Is produced from the soft fibre that grows around the seed of a cotton plant. The Xinjiang area where the desert is produces 84% of China's cotton. India and China are the world's largest producers of cotton.

Cut throat razor. Your dad probably doesn't use one of these to shave in the morning. It's a single long blade that is very sharp and folds into a wooden handle. Called a cut throat because if you are not careful it could cut more than you want!

Day sack. A small rucksack I carried during the day that contained emergency equipment.

Desert Rat. A soldier of the 7th Armoured division, which fought in North Africa during the Second World War. One of the soldiers had a pet jerboa, the general in charge liked the rat so adopted the nickname... Desert Rats! Soldiers like nicknames.

Diplomat. An official like an ambassador who deals with people in a kind and understanding way.

Doppa. An Uyghur word: a square or round skull cap/hat decorated with embroidery.

Drip. A small plastic tube that doctors or nurses put into a vein using a needle. Through this tube medicine and fluids (**intravenous fluid**) can be put into the body of someone who is unwell.

Flares. Like a special firework, it shoots high into the air burning very brightly before gently falling back to earth slowly on a mini parachute. This gives you at least forty seconds of bright light to signal where you are and guide people to you.

Foreign office. A department of the government of the United Kingdom. Responsible for protecting and promoting British interests across the world.

Gestation. How long a baby develops inside its mother's womb before being born. For example: Humans two hundred and sixty-six days, elephants nearly two years and gerbils twenty-two days! Bactrian camel three hundred and ninety-five days.

Global satellite dish. Shaped like an umbrella you will have seen them on the side of some houses. They receive or transmit radio waves to and from satellites. We were using it for mobile phones not TV.

Granny Ola. A delicious breakfast cereal made by Susanna, the artist who illustrated this book.

Hobble. A way of tying one limb up to prevent or limit movement of an animal.

Hotan. This river is formed by the meeting of the white and black jade rivers flowing from the Kunlun Mountains. It carries melted snow and normally only flows during the summer.

Imams. A person who leads prayers; a religious leader of a Muslim community.

Jerboas. Long eared, long tailed, rodents. They have long back legs with tiny bodies and can jump three metres (get your two tallest friends to lie end to end in the school playground and see if you can jump over them... don't squash them!).

Kara-Buran. A violent northeast wind of central Asia. It carries dust and sand and blocks the sun out turning day into night.

Kashgar. An ancient city over two thousand years old, it was an important stop on the Silk Road trading route. Today it is famous for its Sunday bazaar/market.

Kunlun Mountains. Are one of the longest mountain ranges in Asia. Nearly two thousand miles long. The precious stone, Jade, can be found in these sacred mountains.

John Blashford-Snell CBE. Former British Army Officer, explorer and author. Founded Operation Raleigh and the Scientific Exploration Society.

Kindling. Small pieces of dry wood to help start your fire.

Lao Zhao. An important Chinese scientist with extensive knowledge of the desert.

Leonora. Was the daughter of Lord and Lady Romsey. Sadly, age five, Leonora died from a rare kidney cancer. A charity that helped look after children with cancer was set up in her memory.

Libby Purves OBE. British radio presenter, journalist and author.

Long March. During a civil war between nationalists and communist, the Chinese communist army retreated 6000 miles in a year crossing rivers, deserts and mountains an incredibly tough journey that only a few people survived.

Losing face. A cultural understanding of respect, honour and social standing. If you lose face in China people may think less of you.

Mandarin. This is one of the main languages spoken in China.

Mao Suit. A form of national dress worn by men. Usually, a plain dark suit with a high collar and four pockets that represent four virtues of propriety, justice, honesty and shame. Five buttons represent the branches of Chinese government. The Chinese communist leader

Mao Zedong made the suit famous. It is not worn as much today however China's leaders will wear it on important state ceremonies.

Mecca. Birthplace of the prophet Muhammad and Islam's holiest city in western Saudi Arabia. Muslims turn and pray to this religious centre five times a day.

Mirage. A mirage is caused by hot air being at different temperatures. The light bends (refraction) and reflects the blue sky and what you think you see is water!!!! It's a really weird thing.

Miscarriage. A baby animal born before it is able to survive.

Mrs Thatcher. Was the first female prime minister of the United Kingdom from 1979 to 1990. She was given the nickname 'Iron Lady' because of her determination.

Muslim. People who follow and practice Islamic religion. They follow the Quran (Holy Book) and teachings of the Prophet Mohammad.

NASA. (National Aeronautics and Space Administration). United States agency responsible for science and technology in space.

Oasis. A place in a desert where water might be found. Plants may grow and there might even be a town or village.

Oxford Handbook of Clinical Medicine. A fantastic book that presents clear information and guidance on a huge variety of illnesses. Used by doctors and nurses all over the world. Many years later I was privileged to work as a practice nurse for two of the authors; Dr Longmore and Dr Judith Collier. They loved hearing the story of me using their book. Still, to this day, when I open my book sand can be seen between its pages.

Pennant. A long triangular flag attached to military vehicles and ships to identify them.

People's Liberation Army. Is the armed forces of the People's Republic of China and the largest military force in the world.

Presented. I was invited to a party given by the Queen Alexandra's Royal Army Nursing Corps at the Royal Hospital in Chelsea. At the event I was introduced to Princess Margaret. She stood at one end of the red carpet and I was at the other end. She knew a lot about me and the expedition. My old army boss was beside

Princess Margaret, looking anxious. I think she was worried what I was going to say! Of course I behaved!

Queen Alexandra's Royal Army Nursing Corps. Nurses to the British Army and part of the Army Medical services.

Poplar tree. Correct name Populus euphratica. These trees can be very old-some on the edge of the desert are reportedly three thousand years old! They can tolerate salty water and desert conditions. Their long roots will find water deep underground. Leaves turn golden brown in autumn.

Pseudoruminants. Camels are not true ruminants like cows, with four stomachs; camels only have three! Their stomachs act like fermenting chambers with bacteria that help digest tough grain, tamarisk and even an odd sock if you are not careful!!

Rattan woven walls. Rattan is a vine that can be used for weaving. It is very strong, long ago it was used to make walls and helmets for soldiers.

Sand mountain. Charles' name for the huge dunes we came across – some over three hundred metres high. That's as high as sixty cars balancing on top of each other!

Satellite navigation GPS. (Global positioning system). This device gave us a huge advantage over previous explorers, who got lost. The handheld device finds at least four of the thirty satellites high above the earth (16,000 miles away!) These satellites transmit their position constantly and from that your GPS can work out to within a few metres where you are.

Satellite phone. A special mobile phone that connects via radio waves to orbiting satellites. It should work in all areas of planet Earth and is especially useful during natural disasters or expeditions to remote areas.

Sichuan. An area of China that uses a pink peppercorn that is actually the dried fruit from an ash tree. It causes a numbing and tingling sensation on your tongue, it's hot hot hot... but also delicious!

Silk Road. An ancient network of trade routes that connects the East and Western world exchanging goods and ideas.

Sir Ranulph Fiennes OBE. Former British Army Officer and world-renowned polar explorer and author. In 1984 the *Guinness Book of World Records* described him as the world's greatest living explorer.

Silva expedition compass. Produced originally by a company in Sweden, these compasses were used before satellite navigation and are still used today. A compass works because the Earth is a huge magnet. They are always reliable (as long as the person using them knows how to operate it!). A magnetic needle spins freely and will always point towards magnetic north, so you can work out all other directions.

Split grain. The main reason the grain is broken/split is to increase digestibility.

Sven Hedin. 1865–1952 A Swedish geographer, explorer and travel writer.

Sweet well. A way of describing if water is good to drink, sweet water, whilst not sweet, is also not salty.

Taiwan. An island in the western pacific. 100 miles off the coast of southern China. Governed by the Republic of China. Capital city, Taipei.

Taklamakan Desert. Located in North West China. One of the largest sandy deserts in the world.

Tamarisk. A plant that grows in salty deserts and along sea shores; they have very long roots that can find water deep underground.

Telegram. From the Greek words tele = far, graphien = write. A way of sending a written message without the use of an actual letter in the post. Electrical impulses send a coded message down a wire. In 1884 a man from the United States called Morse sent the first telegram. A long time before emails.

The Peoples' Republic of China. The official name for China. It has a population of more than 1.4 billion and covers 5 time zones.

Traditional Chinese Medicine. An ancient approach to healing involving acupuncture, herbal remedies, massage, meditation and restoring balance between yin and yang.

Urumqi. Capital of the Xinjiang Uyghur Autonomous Region. Its name means 'fine pasture' although now it is a major industrial city, rich in mineral resources of oil and coal.

Uyghur. One of China's fifty-five recognised ethnic minorities. They are native to the Xinjiang region of NW China. Primarily Muslim.

Veteran. A person who has been in the military during a war.

World Service. A radio service operated by the British Broadcasting Corporation. Broadcasting news and information in forty different languages all around the world.

The Teams

Charles
Expedition Leader
The adventure was his idea

Rubert (Lotto)
*Crossing team
Navigator
Communications*

Carolyn (Camel Doc)
*Crossing Team
Expedition Medic*
Author of this book

Mark (Kipper)
*Support Team and
Crossing Team
Translator
Communications*

Keith
Professional Photographer

Richard (Little Bean)
Interpreter

Barney
Leader of Support Team

Guo
Chinese Expedition Leader

Zhang
Translator

**Lao Zhao
(Mad Scientist)**
Chef
Expert on the Desert

Esa Polter
Head Camel Handler

Abdul (BP)
Camel Handler

Kirim
Camel Handler

Lucien
Camel Handler

Suleiman
*Became the
Head Camel Handler*
Replaced Esa Polta

Emir (The Poet)
Camel Handler

Rosa
Camel Handler

Fatima
The Only Female Camel
My Friend

Chumba
Leader of the Camels

Thank You to these Awesome People

My family especially my daughters Florence and Lily who encouraged me and never stopped believing. Thank you for the post it notes that fell from the pages of books, or were stuck to my lap top or under my pillow sending love, strength and PAWS UP messages. Simon for your support for many years.

Judith for your continued enthusiasm even after reading and marking the first ideas of a book.

My best friends Fleur and Trace who always made me believe they shared my vision no matter how crazy it seemed.

Patricia and Tony for always being there through some very dark days, for the candles lit and the introduction to the wonderful and healing Holy Island.

Thanks to the honest feedback from my cousin Kate (teacher) and her son Joseph who spurred me on when he said 'it felt like you were reading it just to me!' In life we never realise how important a throwaway line can be to someone.

My lovely next door neighbour Amy who at the school gates said to another mum 'my next-door neighbours writing a children's book.'... and so began an unlikely friendship between Susanna (artist, academic and so much more) her wonderful family and me. Special thanks to Susanna's daughters Anouk and Elfie who could always be relied upon to give honest and yes ... harsh feedback. Seeing little videos that they had made with them laughing at something I had written gave me hope that I might be on to something. Thanks also to dear little Catkin who accepted and eventually really liked going to her child minder so that mummy could get on with drawing.

Sarah and Geoff, old hockey pals from Devon who read the book to their young granddaughter Isla. She drew pictures of camels and apparently couldn't wait to stay with her grandparents to hear more adventures of the Camel doc. Thank you Isla for your excitement and enthusiasm ... I really do exist.

Thanks to my young nieces Scarlet, Nerea and Amelie it's never easy when your aunty keeps asking you to read some rubbish she's written. You were kind but honest the best and only way to lead your life.

Jude and Chas two inspirational teachers that helped my daughters during the early years as they came to terms with dyslexia. Enthusiastically they helped me with spelling and grammar. Thank you both for your patience and positive approach to life.

Like many books it has evolved, originally I wrote it from the perspective of a camel! Even seeking guidance from the great Michael Morpurgo... he was kind enough to send me a hand written post card which I can see stuck on my wall near my lap top. Every word of encouragement helps!

I sent the book out to various agents; I was under no illusion crossing a desert was tough but getting an agent ... well, that's a whole new level of toughness.

I read and re read the Children's Writers' and Artists' Yearbook and followed their guidance. Only one agent Skylark responded with what is known as a positive rejection. I hung onto this tiny bit of light. They wanted me to be brave and write my story not the camels! So began 'Do Explorers Wear Socks.'

Time to think outside the box. I started reading about self-publishing ... not vanity printing but proper self-publishing.

On a visit to Holy Island, I made a detour to York and met with the straight speaking, no nonsense, Duncan of York Publishing Services. Huge thanks go to Duncan, Clare and their team.

Many loyal friends waded through the story trying to help with spelling, grammar and letting me know when things just didn't make sense! Thank you, James, Geoff, Judith, Murray, my neighbour Chrystabell and Peggotty the whippet who let me walk her when my head was spinning from stories of camels and sand storms.

Thanks to Janine and Frankie(dog) for early morning sea swims and for just listening.

St Georges road swim group although you don't see me much your what's app chats have kept me sane and made me laugh lots. You guys didn't even know you were helping.

During the last year I have been walking the South West Coastal path in memory of my brother Keith.

630 miles of the most stunning scenery. Alone on a windswept headland with waves

crashing you can stop, breath and remember how lucky you are. Along the path I met lots of inspiring people and families with young children. We stopped and chatted. I shared my stories with the children. Watching them smile and laugh gave me hope. Those little people and there were lots of you had no idea how much they were helping me.

So really here there has to be a big thank you to the South West Coastal Path to the people, the countryside, nature at its best and most healing … its truly magical and uplifting … even lifesaving.

I am still walking, but hopefully by the time this book is printed I will have completed the 630 miles … I might even do a lap of honour!

Professional help and encouragement came first from Stephanie Baudet (a very successful children's author) Thank you Stephanie for your full and constructive appraisal, for your professional guidance and most importantly your enthusiasm.

Next, I sought guidance from Stephanie Hale of the Oxford Literacy Consultancy (award winning author, journalist and broadcaster).

I braced myself for the return of a full manuscript assessment … scary stuff. To my surprise it was positive, I mean really positive and encouraging, so much so that I thought is this true. Stephanie reassured me, even admitting that she too was surprised and doesn't normally give such a glowing appraisal. Stephanie has been/is amazing responding to my numerous wobbly emails where I am saying HELP what do I do about this. Calm, constructive and encouraging her words are always YOU CAN DO THIS.

Some technical issues with sending the art work required a team effort. Special thanks to a combination of artists and techy people who came to the rescue. Tim, Matt, Susie and Rich you were awesome.

Finally, I would like to thank Charles if he had not chosen me as the Expedition team medic my story and I don't mean just this book would have been very different.

THANK YOU TO YOU ALL ♥